Genders and Sexualities in History

Palgrave Macmillan's series, Genders and Sexualities in History, accommodates and fosters new approaches to historical research in the fields of genders and sexualities. The series promotes world-class scholarship, which concentrates upon the interconnected themes of genders, sexualities, religions/religiosity, civil society, politics and war.

Historical studies of gender and sexuality have, until recently, been more or less disconnected fields. In recent years, historical analyses of genders and sexualities have synthesised, creating new departures in historiography. The additional connectedness of genders and sexualities with questions of religion, religiosity, development of civil societies, politics and the contexts of war and conflict is reflective of the movements in scholarship away from narrow history of science and scientific thought, and history of legal processes approaches, that have dominated these paradigms until recently. The series brings together scholarship from Contemporary, Modern, Early Modern, Medieval, Classical and Non-Western History. The series provides a diachronic forum for scholarship that incorporates new approaches to genders and sexualities in history.

More information about this series at
http://www.palgrave.com/gp/series/15000

Lindsey Earner-Byrne · Diane Urquhart

The Irish Abortion Journey, 1920–2018

palgrave
macmillan

Lindsey Earner-Byrne
School of History
University College Dublin
Dublin, Ireland

Diane Urquhart
Institute of Irish Studies
University of Liverpool
Liverpool, UK

Genders and Sexualities in History
ISBN 978-3-030-03854-0 ISBN 978-3-030-03855-7 (eBook)
https://doi.org/10.1007/978-3-030-03855-7

Library of Congress Control Number: 2018964585

Cover illustration: Pattern adapted from an Indian cotton print produced in the 19th century

This Palgrave Pivot imprint is published by the registered company Springer Nature Switzerland AG
The registered company address is: Gewerbestrasse 11, 6330 Cham, Switzerland

Series Editors' Preface

The Irish Abortion Journey 1920–2018 is a genuinely groundbreaking historical analysis of the marginalisation of women's reproductive rights in Ireland, north and south, since the 1920s and up to the present day. In this highly original and timely book, Lindsey earner-Byrne and Diane Urquhart examine the history of abortions in Ireland, in a context where women's health was consciously side-lined by moral absolutism in both jurisdictions. In an often moving account, the authors explore the development of legal, moral and medical frameworks that excluded legal abortion, and the ways in which some doctors attempted to balance the law against the risks to women's health. This is a history of women in Ireland, north and south, and the startling lack of ownership women had and still have over their bodies. The book traces the harrowing journeys made by women, literally and metaphorically, in the history of abortion in Ireland, often meaning going abroad for help. In common with all volumes in the 'Genders and Sexualities in History' series, *The Irish Abortion Journey 1920–2018* is a multifaceted and meticulously researched scholarly study and is a sophisticated contribution to our understanding of the past.

John Arnold
Sean Brady
Joanna Bourke

Acknowledgements

Our first debt of gratitude is to the many women and men who shared their abortion experiences over the last few years. Their courage and generosity inspired this book. Discussions with colleagues, in particular Deirdre Duffy, Caroline Myerscough, Claire Pierson and participants on the Wellcome-funded Liverpool-Irish Abortion Corridor project, were both instructive and illuminating. To those who have campaigned for change and through the darkest times have continued tirelessly; this book rests upon your resilience and success. It also owes much to the outstanding work produced on Ireland's abortion story for many years by journalists and scholars. Our footnotes and select bibliography hint to the wealth of that work, but it merits mention here too. University College Dublin's Seed Funding initiative supports research into equality, diversity and inclusion and awarded us funding to buy the valuable time we needed to produce this work. Sincere thanks are also due to the following: Lesley Earner-Byrne for proofing this manuscript in draft form and encouraging us that we were on the right track; to John Byrne for valuable practical support; to Dawn Purvis who also read the manuscript in draft form and was more than generous in sharing her wealth of knowledge; to Palgrave, in particular Carmel Kennedy, Emily Russell and Oliver Dyer for not hesitating for a second in embracing this project and offering all the assistance any publisher could to see it over the line; to Derek Speirs who was so generous with his time and photos; to our reader who was insightful, generous and encouraging—we felt a kindred spirit oversaw us in the planning stages. Nicola Morris also proofed and checked the manuscript and made many helpful suggestions. Finally, to our families whose lives were held hostage by this book over the summer of 2018.

Contents

Abbreviations

AAC	Anti-Amendment Campaign
AfC	Alliance for Choice
CAP	Contraception Action Campaign
DHSSPS	Department of Health, Social Services and Public Safety
DUP	Democratic Unionist Party
EC	European Community
ECHR	European Court of Human Rights
FFA	Fatal Foetal Anomaly or Fatal Foetal Abnormalities
HSE	Health Service Executive (Irel)
Iasc	Irish Abortion Solidary Campaign (England)
IFPA	Irish Family Planning Association
IPCC	Irish Pregnancy Counselling Centre
IWASG	Irish Women's Abortion Support Group (England)
IWLM	Irish Women's Liberation Movement
IWU	Irishwomen United
NHS	National Health Service (NI)
NIFPA	Northern Irish Family Planning Association
NILRA	Northern Irish Law Reform Association
NISCBC	Northern Irish Society for Constructive Birth Control
PLAC	Pro-Life Amendment Campaign
SDLP	Social Democratic Labour Party
SPUC	Society for the Protection of the Unborn Child
TFMR	Termination for Medical Reasons [Ireland]
UMJ	*Ulster Medical Journal*
UPAA	Ulster Pregnancy Advisory Association
WRCC	Women's Right to Choose Campaign

List of Figures

List of Tables

Chronology

1861	**Offences Against the Person Act**, sections 58 and 59 criminalised those who conducted and those who procured abortions by the use of poison or instrument
1921	foundation of the **Northern Irish State**
1922	foundation of the **Irish Free State** (known as the Republic of Ireland since 1949)
1929	**Censorship of Publications Act (Irish Free State)** included a prohibition on publications advocating contraceptives; **Adoption of Child Act (NI)**
1930	**Anglican Church's Lambeth Conference resolution 15** permitting restricted access to birth control in 'hard cases' e.g. for married couples when 'there is a morally sound reason for avoiding complete abstinence'
1931	Papal encyclical ***Casti Connubii*** [On Christian Marriage]
1935	**Criminal Law Amendment Act (Irish Free State)** including a prohibition on the sale and importation of contraceptives
1937	**Irish Constitution**—prohibition on divorce and enshrining women's life within the home
1938	***R v Bourne* [1938]** Gynaecologist, Dr. Aleck Bourne, is acquitted of conducting an illegal abortion on the grounds that he performed the abortion on a fourteen-year-old girl as continuance of the pregnancy would have made the girl 'a physical or mental wreck'

1945	**Criminal Justice Act (Northern Ireland)**, section 25 (1) dealt with the crime of 'child destruction' with a penalty of 'penal servitude for life'
1948	extension of **National Health Service** [NHS] to Northern Ireland
1951	**Mother-and-Child Controversy (Republic of Ireland)**
1952	**Adoption Act (Republic of Ireland)** allowed for the adoption of 'illegitimate or orphaned' children residing in the state who were between six months and seven years of age. Under most circumstances the adopters needed to be the same religion as the adoptee's parents (if an orphan) and mother (if 'illegitimate')
1958	***Regina v. Newton and Stungo*** case—Dr. Stungo was found not guilty of performing an illegal abortion on the basis that he had done so in 'good faith' believing the pregnant woman was suicidal. The woman in this case died
1962–1965	**The Second Vatican Council**
1965	***Griswold v Connecticut*** case—American Supreme Court ruled that a state's ban on the use of contraceptives violated a couple's right to marital privacy
1967	**British Abortion Act** which did not extend to Northern Ireland
1968	Papal encyclical ***Humanae Vitae*** [Of Human Life]
1969	beginning of **Northern Ireland conflict**
1971	foundation of **Irish Women's Liberation Movement (Republic of Ireland)**
1972	**Report on the Commission on the Status of Women (Republic of Ireland)**
1973	***Roe v Wade*** **American Supreme Court** ruling; Republic of Ireland and UK **enter EEC**; **Council for the Status of Women [CSW] (Republic of Ireland)** founded; the Irish **High Court rejects Mrs. Mary McGee's case (Republic of Ireland)** against the Attorney General and revenue for seizure of her post (containing birth control)
1974	the **Supreme Court rules in favour of Mrs. Mary McGee (Republic of Ireland)** on the basis that married

couples had the right to make private decisions regarding their family planning; **Irishwomen United [IWU] (Republic of Ireland)** formed

1979 **Health (Family Planning) Act (Republic of Ireland)** restricted sale of birth control to *bona fides* couples (to be defined by a doctor in each case) and stressed that 1861 ban on abortion remained in place; **Women's Right to Choose Group (Republic of Ireland)** established

1983 **Abortion Referendum (Republic of Ireland)** inserts eighth amendment protecting the right to life of the unborn into Irish constitution

1984 **Ann Lovett** and infant die; **Joanne Hayes and Kerry Babies' Tribunal (Republic of Ireland)**

1987 **Hamilton Irish High Court** right to life supersedes right to information

1988 **Irish Supreme Court confirms Hamilton ruling** and made it a crime for service providers to assist women seeking abortions in Britain by either referral or information

1991 Irish government adds **protocol to EU Maastricht Treaty** to ensure it would not 'affect the application in Ireland of Article 40.3.3' referring to the right to the life of the unborn

1992 ***Attorney General v X* [X case] (Republic of Ireland)**—attorney general is granted an injunction by the High Court to prevent a fourteen-year-old rape victim from traveling to the UK for an abortion. **Supreme Court over turns injunction in X case; European Court of Human Rights ruled on Open Door Counselling's appeal** of the Hamilton ruling and found Ireland in breach of the Human Right's Convention's information rights

1992 **twelfth amendment to the Irish constitution referendum** proposed to uphold ban on abortion even in cases of risk of suicide—rejected by the people; **thirteenth amendment to the Irish constitution referendum**—proposed that the abortion ban would limit the freedom of pregnant women to travel out of the state—accepted

	by the people; **fourteenth amendment to the Irish constitution referendum**—proposed that the distribution of information about abortion in foreign countries would not be prohibited—accepted by the people
1993	**The K case (Northern Ireland)** 14-year-old girl in care seeks abortion on the grounds of risk of suicide—courts rule an abortion was in her best interests, but no doctor in Northern Ireland would perform it. K travelled to England for termination
1994	**The A Case (Northern Ireland)**—abortion sought for a twenty-four-year-old with low IQ, judge rules abortion should be available in NI
1995	**The S Case (Northern Ireland)**—a seventeen-year-old woman, described in court as 'mentally handicapped', a gynaecologist and two psychiatrists argued her mental health would be impaired by pregnancy. An abortion was performed in Northern Ireland
1998	**Good Friday Agreement**—a deal ensures the 1967 Abortion Act is not extended to **Northern Ireland**
2001	**Northern Ireland Family Planning Association (NIFPA) initiated legal action against Department of Health, Social Services and Public Safety (DHSSPS)** claiming the latter was failing in its duty to ensure equal access to reproductive health care. NIFPA won right to first judicial review of medical practices relating to abortion and the provision of abortion services in Northern Ireland
2002	**Twenty-fifth amendment to the Irish constitution referendum**—sought to remove threat of suicide, based on X case, as a ground for abortion in Ireland—rejected by the people; NI Judicial Review of DHSSPS and reproductive health care in Northern Ireland High Court
2003	**NI High court ruled DHSSPS** was not failing in its statutory duty, it recommend it provide official guidelines regarding abortion law and practice in NI
2004	NIFPA appealed NI High Court ruling—**Belfast Court of Appeal found DHSSPS had failed in its duties under Article 4 of the Health and Personal Social**

Services of Northern Ireland Order 1972 re. services for women seeking lawful abortions in NI

2005 **DHSSPS begin investigation** into the provision of abortion services in NI

2007 **DHSSPS issue guidelines** on abortion services for consultation; NI Assembly debate and reject those guidelines

2008 **DHSSPS again released guidelines** on abortion services for consultation

2009 **DHSSPS published guidelines** explaining the existing law on abortion in NI; Society for the Protection of the Unborn Child (SPUC) sought judicial review on grounds that the guidelines were illegal; Court ruled the guidelines were not erroneous, but that in relation to non-directive counselling and conscientious objection they failed to give clear guidance and order withdrawal of the document

2010 **Michelle Harte is denied an abortion in Ireland** although ill with cancer; **European Court of Human Rights [ECHR] ruled against Ireland in the *A, B* and *C*** cases on the grounds that Ireland had 'failed to give full effect to the constitutional right of allowing abortion in Ireland where the life of the mother is at risk'; **DHSSPS** released new guidelines on abortion in Northern Ireland but they were not published

2012 Death of **Savita Halappanavar (Republic of Ireland)**; the Irish state settles with **Michelle Harte**, although she had died of cancer

2013 **Protection of Life During Pregnancy Act [PLDPA] (Republic of Ireland)**; **DHSSPS** revises the 2010 abortion guidelines and submits to NI Assembly for consultation; NI Department of Justice confirms it will issue consultation document on abortion law; **NI Human Rights Commission [NIHRC]** advises Department of Justice that existing abortion law violates human rights of women and girls; **Sarah Ewart** goes public re. traveling to England to terminate upon FFA diagnosis

2014 **Miss Y case (Republic of Ireland)** poignantly highlighted the shortcomings of PLDPA; **NI Department of Justice publishes consultation paper** to re. changing

	the law to enable women to choose to terminate a pregnancy in the event of Fatal Foetal Anomaly (FFA); **A & B vs Secretary of State of for Health (UK)** mother and daughter from NI argued in High Court in Manchester that it was discriminatory not to allow NI women abortions funded on the NHS in England. High Court ruled against them
2015	Another **judicial review of DHSSPS abortion guidelines** initiated by legal action taken by a Co. Antrim woman on the grounds that delays had 'compounded the trauma of having an abortion' in NI; NI Minister for Justice indicates intention to seek NI Assembly approval to allow termination of pregnancy in cases of FFA; First Minister of NI rejects Minister for Justice's request and suggests, instead, new guidelines should be drafted
2016	**Woman found guilty in NI under 1861 Offences Against the Person Act** for inducing her own abortion via the use of abortion pills; mother who helped fifteen-year-old daughter to procure abortion pills charged under same act, the mother is challenging prosecution at the time of writing
2017	**Joint Oireachtas Committee on the Eighth Amendment to the Irish Constitution** report supports a referendum to repeal the amendment; UK Supreme Court upheld ban on NHS-funded abortion care in England for women from Northern Ireland; British government introduces new provision to fund abortions in England for Northern Irish women; **Marie Stopes clinic** closes in Belfast
2018	**Referendum to repeal the Eighth Amendment to the Irish constitution**—accepted by the people

CHAPTER 1

Introduction

Abstract This chapter outlines the current position regarding abortion in Northern Ireland and the Republic of Ireland and provides a brief explanation of the history of abortion law in Ireland. It explains why the book adopts a historical and an all-island approach to the analysis of abortion in Ireland arguing that both provide the necessary context required to understand this complex and 'live' issue as part of a broader history of women's health and female agency.

Keywords Abortion · Eighth amendment · Criminalised · Section 58 · Republic of Ireland · Northern Ireland

From 2019, abortion up to twelve weeks gestation will be legal in the Republic of Ireland. It is hard to overestimate the significance of this change, or the irony that the often-lamented socially conservative part of the island has become more liberal than its northern neighbour. Abortion remains illegal in Northern Ireland (except in very narrowly defined circumstances), but the issue is rarely considered either in an all-island or a historical context.[1] While the restrictive nature of abortion

[1] The president of Ireland signed the bill to repeal the eighth amendment to the Irish constitution on 18 September 2018. Legislation is still to follow. F. Kelly, 'President Signs Bill Repealing Eighth Amendment into Law', *Irish Times*, 18 September 2018.

L. Earner-Byrne and D. Urquhart, *The Irish Abortion Journey, 1920–2018*, Genders and Sexualities in History,
https://doi.org/10.1007/978-3-030-03855-7_1

law on the island of Ireland has made it anomalous in Western Europe, it is in fact in keeping with the conservative nature of both jurisdictions, in particular, in relation to the status of women, reproductive rights and sexual morality. The abortion question is often reduced to a 'Catholic issue' in the Republic and a rallying point of rare political consensus in Northern Ireland, but neither interpretation fully reflects the complexity of the history of the Irish abortion journey. This book considers the history of Irish abortion against a broader backdrop of female agency since the foundation of both states on the island of Ireland to the present day. It disentangles the tropes and myths, which have been recycled and rehashed since the earliest discussions on women's sexuality and reproduction in Ireland, and considers why some of these still endure.

The Legal Framework

Since the mid-twentieth century there has been a period of transnational abortion reform with 'a wave of amendments ... where most countries spell out exceptions under which induced abortion is not subject to penalties'.[2] Reform was, for example, introduced in the Soviet Bloc, Western and Central Asia and Eastern, Northern and Southern Europe in the early- to mid-1950s and in the developed and developing world including China, Cuba, India and Tunisia in the 1960–1970s. By the mid-1980s abortion was legal in most of Europe and North America and from 1985 to 2010 nearly all remaining European countries removed restrictions alongside South Africa, Cambodia, Nepal, Vietnam, Guyana and Mexico. Collectively this amounted to a 'slow and steady historical shift', but the reform process was not universal. Andorra, Malta and San Marino were the only developed regions without provision for abortion alongside twenty-three countries in developing regions and as a recent world report on access to safe abortion noted: 'Abortion is explicitly permitted in only the most dire of circumstances – when needed to save a woman's life – in 39 countries; of those, only (Ireland) is in the developed world'.[3]

Abortion was not unknown in eighteenth and nineteenth-century Ireland, but it was seemingly uncommon and closely associated with

[2] S. Singh, L. Remez, G. Sedgh, L. Kwok, and T. Onda, *Abortion Worldwide 2017 Uneven Progress and Unequal Access* (New York: Guttmacher Institute, 2018), p. 14.

[3] Ibid., p. 15.

single motherhood, shame and surreptitious procedures.[4] As the historian, Kenneth H. Connell suggested, 'Abortion ... was no matter for general discussion: the slenderness ... of the evidence probably indicates the rarity of the practice'.[5] Abortion was, however, sufficiently worrying to legislators and moralists to prompt the passage of the Offences Against the Person Act of 1861, section 58 of which read:

> Every woman, being with child, who, with intent to procure her own miscarriage, shall unlawfully administer to herself any poison or other noxious thing, or shall unlawfully use any instrument or other means whatsoever with the like intent, and whosoever, with intent to procure the miscarriage of any woman, whether she be or be not with child, shall unlawfully administer to her or cause to be taken by her any poison or other noxious thing, or shall unlawfully use any instrument or other means whatsoever with the like intent, shall be guilty of felony, and being convicted thereof shall be liable ... to be kept in penal servitude for life.

Section 59 of the act criminalised those who assisted with an abortion and 'unlawfully supply or procure any poison or other noxious thing...with the intent to procure the miscarriage of any woman, whether she be or be not with child, shall be guilty of a misdemeanour'.[6] This act covered the island of Ireland as a constituent part of the UK at the time of its passage and it remained in force following the partition of Ireland in 1921.[7]

The Historical Framework

The creation of the state of Northern Ireland in 1921 and the establishment of the Irish Free State in 1922 allowed both parts of the island to forge their own policies in relation to sexuality and reproductive

[4] K. H. Connell, *Irish Peasant Society* (Oxford: Oxford University Press, 1968), pp. 62–63.

[5] Ibid., p. 245.

[6] For the full text of these sections see, Offences against the Person Act, 1861 on the Irish Statute Book website, http://www.irishstatutebook.ie/eli/1861/act/100/section/58/enacted/en/html. Also available on, https://www.legislation.gov.uk/ukpga/Vict/24-25/100/section/58.

[7] Ireland was partitioned under the Government of Ireland Act, 1920, which came into force on 3 May 1921.

issues.[8] The religious make-up of both states was very different; the Irish Free State was overwhelmingly Roman Catholic and the Northern Irish State was made up of a majority of Protestant religions (mainly Presbyterian, Church of Ireland and Methodists) and a significant minority of Roman Catholics.[9] The tendency in political discourse and scholarship has been to accentuate and focus on those differences, however, this book is equally interested in what both parts of the island shared. Socially, there was, in fact much common ground until at least the 1990s. The island of Ireland was overwhelmingly Christian conservative and religion was considered a vital attribute of identity for much of the twentieth century. Although there were differences in degree and inflection between the denominations on the island, there was also much agreement in relation to sexual morality and other social issues. Crucially, there was a strongly held conviction that faith should inform social values and state policy. This book explores how a conservative moral climate came to dominate decision-making in relation to legislation concerning women and sexuality in both states on the island. Throughout the 1920s and 1930s, as Britain embarked on a path of gradual liberalisation in relation to issues such as birth control and divorce,[10] both jurisdictions in Ireland

[8]Northern Ireland was created by the Government of Ireland Act of 1920 and comprises the six north-eastern Ulster counties of Antrim, Armagh, Down, Fermanagh, Londonderry/Derry and Tyrone. Although Northern Ireland remains part of the United Kingdom, it can reject its laws on a limited basis. The Irish Free State, comprising the remaining twenty-six counties on the island, was provided with dominion status under the Anglo-Irish Treaty of 1921. For more detailed information see, S. J. Connolly, *The Oxford Companion to Irish History* (Oxford: Oxford University Press, 1998), pp. 390–92, p. 268.

[9]The first census of the Irish Free State recorded a total population of 2,971,992 of which 2,751,269 was Roman Catholic. Northern Ireland's census was held on the same day in 1926 and recorded a total population of 1,256,561 of which 653,029 belonged to one of the main Protestant faiths (Presbyterian, 300,101; Church of Ireland, 303,374 and Methodist, 49,554) and 420,428 to the Roman Catholic church. For the Irish Free State, see, Department of Industry and Commerce, *Soarstát Éireann, Census of Population, 1926, Volume III: Part 1 Religions* (Dublin, 1926), p. 1; For Northern Ireland see, Table 27: Religious Professions, *Census 1926: Northern Ireland, General Report* (Belfast: HMSO, 1926), p. 57.

[10]L. Hall, *Sex, Gender and Social Change in Britain Since 1880* (London: Red Globe Press, 2000); H. Cook, *The Long Sexual Revolution: English Women, Sex and Contraception, 1800–1975* (Oxford: Oxford University Press, 2004), pp. 113–21.

consciously battened down the moral hatches.[11] While the two nascent states began crafting identities based, in part at least, on difference and hostility to one another, they also came to reflect each other's anxieties in relation to rising crime and violence, ebbing moral standards, decreasing parental control and increasing sexual promiscuity. People who deviated from the stringent moral codes pertaining in both states had limited options and often found themselves ostracised, incarcerated and exiled. Indeed, many exercised the limited agency they had and migrated. This book charts the historical roots of this moral intolerance and its impact on women's health. In particular, it explores how the treatment of unmarried mothers in both parts of the island reflected the status of all women and their bodily autonomy. At its most pernicious this was a divide and conquer morality; 'legitimate' and 'illegitimate' women, implicitly and sometimes explicitly, were pitched against each other and all women were potentially endangered by the prioritisation of morality over health.[12]

This book examines how and why women's health was consciously sidelined in Ireland from the beginning of the reproductive debates in the 1920s. It reveals how it was fully understood by contemporaries that the cost of moral absolutism in relation to birth control, and later abortion, would cost some women their lives. This study also explores how both states implicitly acknowledged that the maintenance of restrictive legislation in relation to abortion was only possible because women themselves sought solutions to unwanted, unviable or damaging pregnancies in other jurisdictions. Although the Irish abortion trail is now geographically diverse, for decades Britain was the necessary alter ego of two states unwilling to confront the consequences of their illusions of moral superiority.[13] Similarly, the export of its women, while

[11] D. Urquhart, *A History of Irish Divorce* (Cambridge: Cambridge University Press, forthcoming 2019).

[12] The papal encyclical *Casti Connubii* (1931), for example, condemned the: 'inversion of the true order of things, ready and bountiful assistance provided to the unmarried mother and her illegitimate offspring (who, of course must be helped in order to avoid a greater evil) which is denied to legitimate mothers'. Cited in A. Fremantle, *The Papal Encyclicals in Their Historical Context* (New York: The New American Library, 1956), p. 242.

[13] The Netherlands has, for example, emerged as a key site on the Irish abortion trail.

acknowledged as 'humiliating' as early as the 1940s, did not cause much official concern in either part of Ireland.[14]

However, despite the severe restrictions on the availability of abortion on the island of Ireland, this book explores the history of the abortions, both legal and illegal, which were performed in Ireland. It considers what is known regarding illegal abortions and what this tells us about women's agency and lack thereof. It also analyses how medical understandings of therapeutic abortions—abortions performed due to medical necessity—were influenced by the wider social and cultural understandings of morality. In this respect, the book focuses, in particular, on the role of doctors and what was understood by the concept of 'good faith' abortions. It is evident that medics in both states were constantly negotiating the balance between the law and 'acceptable' risks to women's health throughout this period. While in both states religion was a constant factor, in Northern Ireland a particularly delicate balance had to be struck and it will be contended here that this was a vital factor in the decision not to extend the 1967 Abortion Act to the region. In fact, the abortion act offered both states the opportunity to savour outrage, while looking the other way as Britain provided these medical services to Irish women. Indeed, this book highlights how, not only was the impact of illegal abortions and abortion travel on women's health and wellbeing rarely considered, both states actually worked to make these journeys harder.

Women and their bodies are central to this history. Women are, of course, not homogenous and are often divided by religion, ethnicity, class, age and ideology. There were women who waved the flag for patriarchy, who righteously punished those who transgressed, and many more who ignored the reality of a restrictive abortion regime. However, all women were confined by the power structures that underpinned two relatively authoritarian states and two societies tinged with fundamentalism for much of the twentieth century.[15] No woman owned her own body as long as she did not have the legal right to control what happened to it. For many women this was an accepted reality and joy was found in

[14]A phrase repeatedly used in relation to Irish unmarried mothers who migrated to Britain. See Chapter 2.

[15]For an exploration of these power structures see, L. Earner-Byrne, *Letters of the Catholic Poor: Poverty in Independent Ireland, 1920–1940* (Cambridge: Cambridge University Press, 2017), pp. 211–51.

the children birthed and raised. For others this was a life sentence. Many faced relentless pregnancies, others, ill with tuberculosis bloomed temporarily in pregnancy's first flush, only to die when their babies were not yet weaned.[16] Others faced pregnancies born of domestic violence and/or rape and were trapped with few options. However, what emerges strongly from this study is the role of female networks in filling the fissures left by state denial of women's bodily autonomy. This book traces the many ways in which the history of abortion in Ireland is a woman's journey: women were confidantes, abortionists, volunteers, campaigners and witnesses.

The Reformist Framework

Finally, this is a history of reform, of what prevents it and what makes it possible. It is an irony that the Republic of Ireland provided the more fertile ground for reform partially due to the energies of conservative anti-abortion forces. It is argued here that the insertion of the eighth amendment into the Irish Republic's constitution in 1983, which protected the life of the unborn and resulted in a complete ban on abortion unless the mother's life was in imminent danger, and the campaign that preceded it, forced Ireland to confront the issue of abortion. For the first time there was a public space for a discussion of the consequences of Ireland's restrictive regime. Some defended it passionately, insisting it must be protected in the constitution, others decried it as hypocrisy and highlighted the trail of women leaving the state each day to procure abortions in Britain. The Republic of Ireland was to continue talking abortion for the next thirty years resulting in five more abortion-related referendums between 1992 and 2018.[17] However, in Northern Ireland there was no such arena for debate, there were no referendums and much of the decision-making did not include the public. This book therefore compares the treatment of the abortion issue in both states throughout the warring 1970s and 1980s, when relations between

[16] This was a common pattern observed of women with pulmonary tuberculosis. See, Chapters 2 and 3.

[17] After the initial referendum in 1983, there were three referendums in 1992, one in 2002 and one in 2018.

the two states were extremely poor, and into the era of the peace process.[18] Throughout this period the two states warily watched each other, aware they were increasingly isolated in their stance in relation to abortion. While the states found little solidarity in each other's company, the women of the island who needed abortions or wanted to support those who did increasingly began to compare notes. The large public protests throughout the 1990s and 2000s after various abortion cases and tragic deaths helped to transform a sense of shame into a slow-burning anger across the island.

In 2016, the stark Twitter feed of two Irish women travelling to Britain to access abortion services was symptomatic of the lessening of secrecy, shame and stigma. Women now demanded that their lived experience of the Irish abortion journey be heard:

> Two Women, one procedure, 48 hours away from home…secrecy, panic and guilt…[in] a series of waiting rooms, moments in transit, a sequence of teduims protracted by stigma…[19]

Like so many travelling for abortion, they remained anonymous, but their use of Twitter allowed the Irish abortion trail to be followed in 'real time', publicising and humanising the ordeal of abortion travel in equal measure. This was also a political act to highlight the need for legislative reform on the island of Ireland; their individual journey was consciously portrayed as part of a longer history of female moral export. They travelled 'in stern solidarity with all our Irish sisters who have gone before us'.[20] It was only when women like this determined to tell the stories of their abortion journeys that the dynamic changed. This book is a testament to how incredibly difficult and radicalising that process has been on the island of Ireland.

[18]The conflict in Northern Ireland, popularly known as 'the troubles', occurred between 1969 and 1998. The peace process era is generally regarded as having commenced in early 1990s and culminated in the Good Friday Agreement of April 1998.

[19]The woman, accompanied by a female friend, travelled from Ireland to the UK for an abortion on 22 August 2016. They live tweeted about their experience, http://www.independent.co.uk/news/uk/abortion-ban-ireland-woman-live-tweets-journey-twitter-a7200916.html, accessed 5 October 2017.

[20]Ibid.

CHAPTER 2

Maternity and Moral Migration, 1920s–1960s

Abstract Since the legalisation of abortion in Britain in 1967, an estimated 200,000 women have travelled from the island of Ireland to England for the termination of a pregnancy. However, the origins of the Irish abortion trail are at least a century old and lie in women emigrating to Britain to flee the moral intolerance that pertained in Ireland towards unmarried mothers and their offspring. The emigration of Irish pregnant single mothers since at least the 1920s allowed both states and conservative commentators to boast of low illegitimacy rates and high moral purity. This chapter traces this early history and explores moral migration in the context of growing concern regarding the impact of repeated pregnancies and maternal health more generally. In particular, the tension that developed between contemporary concerns for public morality and women's health is assessed.

Keywords Abortion trail · Termination · Morality · Emigration · Single mothers · Illegitimacy

Since the legalisation of abortion in Britain in 1967, an estimated 200,000 women have travelled from the island of Ireland to England for

L. Earner-Byrne and D. Urquhart, *The Irish Abortion Journey, 1920–2018*, Genders and Sexualities in History,
https://doi.org/10.1007/978-3-030-03855-7_2

the termination of a pregnancy.[1] However, the origins of the Irish abortion trail are at least a century old and lie in women emigrating to Britain to flee the moral intolerance that pertained in Ireland towards unmarried mothers and their offspring. Such a move was initially more commonly prompted by a desire to hide a pregnancy or seek an adoption than a termination, but it underlines the duration and complexity of this movement.[2] Just as Irish society, until very recently, denied the reality of Irish abortions because they happened outside the jurisdiction, the emigration of Irish pregnant single mothers since at least the 1920s allowed both states and conservative commentators to boast of low illegitimacy rates and high moral standards.[3] This chapter traces this early history and explores maternal migration in the context of growing concern regarding the impact of repeated pregnancies on maternal health. In particular, the tension that developed between contemporary concerns about public morality and women's health is assessed.

Cultures of Shame

After the political independence of southern Ireland in 1922, a self-conscious narrative of moral superiority emerged to differentiate the fledgling state from its erstwhile coloniser.[4] An active laity, various

[1]The Irish Family Planning Association calculates that from 1980 to 2017 at least 173,308 women travelled from the Republic of Ireland to the UK for abortions, www.ifpa/Hot-Topics/Abortion/Statistics, accessed 2 September 2018. These estimates do not include women from Ireland who travelled to other countries, for example, the Netherlands.

[2]P. Jackson, 'Outside the Jurisdiction: Irishwomen Seeking Abortion', in C. Curtin, P. Jackson, and B. Connor (eds), *Gender in Irish Society* (Galway: Galway University Press, 1987), pp. 203–23.

[3]L. Earner-Byrne, 'The Boat to England: An Analysis of the Official Reactions to the Emigration of Single Expectant Irishwomen to Britain, 1922–1972', *Irish Economic and Social History Journal*, 30 (2003), pp. 52–70; L. McCormick, *Regulating Sexuality: Women in Twentieth-Century Northern Ireland* (Manchester: Manchester University Press, 2009).

[4]M. Finnane, 'The Carrigan Committee of 1930–1931 and the "Moral Condition of the Saorstát"', *Irish Historical Studies*, 23:128 (November 2001), pp. 519–36; S. McAvoy, 'The Regulation of Sexuality in the Irish Free State', in E. Malcolm and G. Jones (eds), *Medicine, Disease and the State in Ireland, 1650–1940* (Cork: Cork University Press, 1999), pp. 253–66; J. Smith, 'The Politics of Sexual Knowledge: The Origins of Ireland's Containment Culture and the Carrigan Report (1931)', *Journal of the History of Sexuality*, 13:2 (2004), pp. 208–33; M. Gialanella Valiulis, 'Virtuous Mothers

professional groups, religious leaders and politicians worked hard to shape independent Ireland's society and legislation in accordance with Catholic moral teaching.[5] While this discourse was explicitly Catholic, there was similar moral anxiety reflected in the writings of other faiths until at least the 1960s. As Chrystal Hug notes, 'the ideal of social purity [was] a Victorian prerogative as much as a Catholic one, there were nonetheless differences in degree and in the means employed'.[6] This buttressing moral conservatism explains the striking similarities between the attitudes of the main Protestant denominations and Catholic morality. In consequence, very similar views of unmarried motherhood and morality pertained in Northern Ireland.

In both states shame and secrecy formed fundamental bulwarks of societies which placed a high premium on sexual 'purity'. There is considerable evidence of the social intolerance of sex outside marriage and, in particular, of the shunning of unmarried mothers. That Irish unmarried mothers from both jurisdictions believed that a ship to England was preferable to facing the social stigma at home was acknowledged since the beginning of public discourse on the subject in the early twentieth century.[7] In 1922, a writer using the pen name 'Sagart' (the Irish for priest) explained the predicament of unmarried women who discovered they were pregnant:

and Dutiful Wives: The Politics of Sexuality in the Irish Free State', in M. Gialanella Valiulis (ed.), *Gender and Power in Irish History* (Dublin: Irish Academic Press, 2009), pp. 100–14.

[5] Curtis goes so far as to argue that these forces were so concerted that they represented a challenge to democracy. See M. Curtis, *A Challenge to Democracy: Militant Catholicism in Ireland* (Dublin: The History Press, 2010). See also, S. McAvoy, '"Its Effect on Public Morality Is Vicious in the Extreme": Defining Birth Control as Obscene and Unethical, 1926–1932', in E. Farrell (ed.), *'She Said She Was in the Family Way': Pregnancy and Infancy in Modern Ireland* (London: The Institute of Historical Research, 2012), pp. 35–52.

[6] C. Hug, *The Politics of Sexual Morality in Ireland* (Basingstoke and New York: Macmillan Press, 1999), p. 3.

[7] See, for example, Rev. R. S. Devane, S.J., 'The Unmarried Mother: Some Legal Aspects of the Problem: I', *Irish Ecclesiastical Record*, 23 (1924), pp. 55–68; Rev. R. S. Devane, S.J., 'The Unmarried Mother: Some Legal Aspects of the Problem: II', *Irish Ecclesiastical Record*, 23 (1924), pp. 172–88; Rev. R. S. Devane, S.J., 'The Unmarried Mother and the Poor Law Commission', *Irish Ecclesiastical Record*, 31 (1928), pp. 561–82; Rev. R. S. Devane, S.J., 'The Legal Protection of Girls', *Irish Ecclesiastical Record*, 37 (1931), pp. 20–40.

> Such a girl is smitten with a panic and fear of exposure, and under the pretext of illness, operation, vacation, visiting friends, etc., runs away from her home. She may come up to Dublin from the country, or, if she be a Dublin girl, may go to a distant part of the city, or she may go across to England. In all these cases she runs extreme danger.[8]

The danger 'Sagart' had in mind was to a woman's moral rather than her physical or mental wellbeing. The bastion of Anglicism in Ireland, *The Irish Times*, also lamented that, despite censorship laws that particularly targeted English papers, the Irish media was forced to deal daily with 'wicked and disgusting' subjects. In a tone repeated in all major contemporary reports on welfare and society in Ireland during this period,[9] the paper suggested that 'every honest Irishman must admit that the country's reputation is in danger':

> Infanticide is common – one judge has described it as "a national industry" – and the reports of cases in which unmarried mothers have been brought to trial for this crime indicate a general looseness of manners, a contempt of moral decencies, that are a wholly new feature of Irish life.[10]

For many contemporaries the unmarried mother was representative of declining moral standards and the response was to consign her to 'homes' or Britain. In both jurisdictions these homes were often old workhouses, in which the majority of unmarried mothers resided, or Magdalene asylums that predated partition.[11] In addition, Catholic nuns ran various mother-and-baby homes throughout Ireland, some of which

[8] Sagart, 'How to Deal with the Unmarried Mother', *The Irish Ecclesiastical Record*, 20 (July–December 1922), pp. 145–53, p. 146.

[9] See, for example, *Report of the Committee on Evil Literature* (Dublin, 1927); Commission on the Relief of the Sick and Destitute Poor, *Report of Committee on the Relief of the Sick and Destitute Poor* (Dublin, 1927); *Report of the Committee on the Criminal Law Amendments Acts (1880–1885)*; Commission on Emigration, *Report of the Commission on Emigration and Other Population Problems, 1948–1954* (Dublin, 1956).

[10] 'Irish Morals', *Irish Times*, 2 March 1929.

[11] M. Luddy, 'Moral Rescue and Unmarried Mothers in Ireland in the 1920s', *Women's Studies*, 30 (2001), pp. 797–817. As well as county homes, special homes were opened and administered by poor law authorities, but run by religious orders for example in Pelletstown, Dublin.

remained in operation until the 1980s.[12] The Legion of Mary, a Catholic organisation, also ran homes for unmarried mothers in Dublin and Belfast while the Salvation Army and other Protestant charities operated refuges or hostels for unmarried mothers.[13] At the heart of this system was class and religious prejudice, both of which were reflected outside these institutions by the ways in which unmarried mothers and their children were treated. Since the 1930s, the Irish government admitted that these old workhouses, known as County Homes, were not suitable locations for unmarried mothers stating that: 'It is now generally recognised that unmarried mothers should not remain for long in the County Homes'. However, the real fear was that 'unless active measures designed to enable them to return eventually to the work-a-day world are taken at the critical time, they are in danger of becoming a permanent burden on the ratepayers or drifting into a life of degradation'.[14] While the 'care' of these women was often couched in religious and moral terms, financial considerations were central.[15] In reality, unmarried mothers were often held for years in an exploitive environment working for free and their children languished in institutions dying at truly staggering rates.[16]

As early as the 1920s there was concern in Ireland about the agency, albeit limited, that single pregnant Irish women were exercising by either

[12] In the south the Sacred Heart Order ran the Manor House Mother and Baby Home at Castlepollard in Westmeath between 1935 and 1971. In Northern Ireland, the Good Shepherd Sisters ran Marianville Home for Mothers and Babies in Belfast. In the Republic, the treatment of women in these homes and, in particular, the issue of infant mortality at these homes is currently the subject of an official commission. See Department of Children and Youth Affairs, *Report of the Inter-department Group on Mother and Baby Homes* (July 2014), https://www.dcya.gov.ie/documents/publications/20140716InterdepartReport-MothBabyHomes.pdf, accessed 20 February 2018. Since 2103 Amnesty has pushed for an inquiry into mother and baby homes in Northern Ireland. See, for example http://data.nicva.org/article/mother-and-baby-homes-case-public-inquiry. In response the Northern Ireland Executive is currently funding research into the main homes.

[13] The Salvation Army ran, for example, Thorndale House, Belfast.

[14] Report of the Department of Local Government and Public Health, 1930–1931 (1932), National Archives, Ireland [hereafter NAI], Taoiseach Files, S8345.

[15] For an explanation of the class basis of this system see, L. Earner-Byrne, *Mother and Child: Maternity and Child Welfare in Dublin, 1922–1960* (Manchester: Manchester University Press, 2007), p. 185.

[16] For Northern Ireland see, http://data.nicva.org/dataset/milltown-cemetery-1942-infant-death-and-burial-records. For the Republic see, Earner-Byrne, *Mother and Child*, pp. 195–207.

refusing to enter institutions and fleeing to urban centres like Dublin or Belfast or by emigrating to Britain or further afield. Irish commentators, religious and charity workers and politicians soon began to fret over the numbers of pregnant Irish women who chose to leave the island to escape the incarceratory regimes there. In 1924 Florence Russell of the Liverpool and County Catholic Aid Society wrote to the Catholic Archbishop of Dublin of the 'large number of girls who have come from Ireland on the streets of Liverpool', pointing out that these 'fallen Irish girls are turned out of their country to be supported by English charity'. There was not much female solidarity expressed, as Russell noted, 'we Irish women workers are ashamed of these girls; they bring disgrace on our religion and our country'.[17] However, this must be understood in the light of the relatively vulnerable position of all Irish immigrants in Britain at this time, and Irish women in particular, who were often subjected to hostility in their host country and suspicion from their home country.[18]

By 1930, the English Catholic hierarchy contacted the Irish government urging official action to prevent this prenatal outflow of Irish women and this resulted in a rather haphazard repatriation scheme that prioritised the return of infants conceived in Ireland but born in Britain.[19] However, there is little evidence that this scheme had any real impact on the emigration of pregnant Irish women. The case of one unmarried pregnant woman from Clonakilty in County Cork is revelatory of the potential implications of this official tug-of-war: resident in London in 1940, she was treated for haemorrhage in June and promptly returned to Ireland where she gave birth in July. Upon arrival, she became distraught when she released she had been misled in London where she had been promised she would be dealt with in Dublin far from people who might know her. Quite apart from the risks to her health of travelling after a haemorrhage only to give birth weeks later, she was forced to return to her local area where her anonymity was not

[17] Florence Russell, Hon. Sec. of the Liverpool and County Catholic Aid Society to Archbishop Byrne, June 1924. Cited in L. Earner-Byrne, 'The Boat to England', p. 60.

[18] J. Redmond, 'Sinful Singleness? Discourses on Irish Women's Emigration to England, 1922–1948', *Women's History Review*, 17 (2008), pp. 455–76.

[19] Earner-Byrne, 'The Boat to England', pp. 52–70; P. M. Garrett, 'The Abnormal Flight: Migration and Repatriation of Irish Unmarried Mothers', *Social History*, 25 (2000), pp. 330–43.

guaranteed.[20] This is indicative of how little emphasis was placed on women and their health, both physical and mental, at the centre of this history: the British wanted rid of her and the Irish offered her a system that terrified her and a society that rejected her and her infant. Writing in 1936 the journalist Gertrude Gaffney saw no irony in condemning Irish unmarried mothers in Britain because they gave 'decent Irish girls an unenviable name, and our country an unenviable reputation', while also citing a British-based nun who had described these women as 'scapegoats of a tradition of puritanism that will not admit that things are as they are'.[21] Gaffney's own views clearly reflected the very attitudes she scrutinised.

For its part, the Irish government was also more embarrassed than concerned by the movement of pregnant women to Britain. When addressing the continued complaints from Britain towards the end of the Second World War, the Irish Minister for External Affairs, noted that this migration of Irish pregnant women to Britain was 'humiliating for the country'.[22] Although, the women caught in the official crossfire barely featured in the debates, writing in 1948, the Department of Local Government and Public Health Inspector, Alice Litster highlighted the lack of facilities for unmarried mothers and their children in Ireland, asking: 'What have we to offer her here in comparison with the concealment, comfort and facility for adoption in Great Britain'?[23] There was no adoption regulation in southern Ireland until 1952—delayed largely due to religious concerns that Catholic infants could be adopted by Protestant parents—as a result the unmarried mother often had to rely on private adoption for which she paid exorbitant fees to 'fixers' who made the arrangements.[24] Some women struggled to keep their children

[20] Memo from A. Litster, 13 June 1940. NAI: Clandillon Papers, Box (3). Letters/Reports setting up of Repatriation Scheme UK/Ireland, 1939–1950.

[21] G. Gaffney, 'The Girl Emigrant', *Irish Independent*, 15 December 1936.

[22] Memo. for Taoiseach from J. P. Walsh re. travel permits, 9 April 1944, NAI, Taoiseach Files, S11582B.

[23] A. Litster, 'Unmarried Mother, in Great Britain and at Home', 8 May 1948, *Implementation of the Children's Acts, 1945–1951*, NAI, Clandillon Papers, Box (3). This section was deleted by the internal censor from the final report.

[24] Saint Patrick's Guild had a long history in organising such adoptions and charged extremely high fees to the unmarried mother. M. J. Maguire, *Precarious Childhood in Post-Independence Ireland* (Manchester: Manchester University Press, 2009), pp. 78, 92. The fee could range from £20 in the 1920s rising to £50 in the 1930s. L. Earner-Byrne, 'The Rape of Miss Mary M.: A Mircrohistory of Sexual Violence and Moral Redemption in

born outside marriage, but faced huge obstacles. In 1946, one woman had the courage to apply through the courts for the return of her 'illegitimate' daughter, which she claimed had been adopted against her will. In fact, this baby had been sold and illegally registered in the adopted parents' name meaning it was impossible in most cases for the birth mother to be traced.[25]

In Northern Ireland, as Leanne McCormick notes, 'across the class divide, pregnancy outside marriage carried a great stigma', thus 'rescue homes provided an important service in removing a problem child from the family domicile'.[26] Although adoption was legislated for in England and Wales in 1926, this was not extended to Northern Ireland until 1929, when the Adoption of Children Act (NI) was enacted.[27] By the 1940s placing a child for adoption became the preferred option of many middle-class Northern Irish women while only 10% of babies adopted came from the 'care system'.[28] However, indicative of the religious anxieties that dogged attempts to introduce adoption legislation was the fact that, uniquely in the UK, in Northern Ireland it was, and still is, permissible for a birth parent to specify the religion in which they would like a child being placed for adoption to be raised.[29] The inadequacies of the system resulted in heartbreaking advertisements appearing in newspapers such as the following from 1948: 'WOULD some kind person

1920s Ireland', *Journal of the History of Sexuality*, 24 (January 2015), pp. 75–98. By the 1940s the fees had reached £70. See 'Mother's Application Adjourned', *Irish Examiner*, 5 June 1946. Adoption was increasingly common in Europe in the 1950s.

[25] 'Mother's Application', *Irish Examiner*, 5 June 1946. After sustained coverage on the issue, in particular by journalist Conall Ó Fátharta, the Irish Adoption Authority is currently examining the illegal registration of adopted children. C. Ó Fátharta, 'Illegal Adoptions Known to HSE Since 2012', *Irish Examiner*, 23 April 2018. See also, M. Milotte, *Banished Babies: The Secret History of Ireland's Baby Export Business* (Dublin: New Island Books, 1997).

[26] McCormick, *Regulating Sexuality*, p. 55.

[27] See http://www.bbc.co.uk/news/uk-northern-ireland-24819518, accessed 22 April 2018.

[28] See also, Northern Irish Assembly, 'Research and Library Service Briefing: Overview of Adoption' (paper 126/10), 29 August 2010, p. 2.

[29] Ibid.

adopt Baby Boy, 2 years old; or would pay 10/- per week. R.C. [Roman Catholic]. Box 3249 "Ulster Herald" Office. Omagh'.[30]

It was also clear that 'illegitimate' children were accorded a shockingly low status in both states. In 1927, a case of abuse came before the courts in Belfast in which an adoptive mother had badly beaten a boy in her care. Her defence was that she had lost contact with his mother and was no longer receiving any money for his maintenance.[31] Three years later the *Offaly Independent* recounted a similar tale of the treatment of such a child in the south:

> a child of eight years, when found…weighed only thirty-two pounds. He was taken from the custody of his step-father and indifferent mother. The boy was an illegitimate child of the woman, therefore, the "unwanted" one. His body was a mass of sores, wounds and bruises and while the remainder of the family slept on a bed, he was compelled to sleep the long winter nights through on a wet sack on a damp bedroom floor.[32]

There were also regular reports throughout Ireland—north and south—of the 'stealthy slaughter' of 'unwanted' babies by baby farmers (people who fostered children for money).[33] This treatment of unmarried mothers and their children in Ireland clearly indicates that the hostility to the idea of abortion was often less about a concern for the unborn than it was about notions of morality.

Maternal Health Versus Morality

Ireland's peculiar demography should also be borne in mind when considering its history of reproductive rights: Irish people from the mid-nineteenth century traditionally married late and, even with a more limited period of wifely fertility, the marital birth rate was very high in comparison to other Western European countries.[34] Later marriage and

[30] *Ulster Herald*, 5 June 1948. There are many of these adverts, see, for example: *Ulster Herald*, 26 April 1948; *Anglo-Celt*, 13 July 1946; 22 November 1947; 15 May 1948.

[31] 'Woes of an Unwanted Child', *Irish Independent*, 20 July 1927.

[32] 'Work of the NSPCC', *Offaly Independent*, 22 November 1930.

[33] 'Protection of the Innocents', *Irish Press*, 4 November 1932.

[34] For an excellent review of demography and women see, M. E. Daly, 'Marriage, Fertility and Women's Lives in Twentieth-Century Ireland (c.1900–c.1970)', *Women's History Review*, 15:4 (September 2006), pp. 571–85. High levels of marriage and martial fertility were sustained in Northern Ireland until the middle of the twentieth century, but

multiple pregnancies left Irish married women particularly vulnerable to the risks of childbirth and foetal abnormalities. Important demographic differences, however, emerged between the north and the south of the country. After 1921, for example, the high birth rate in Northern Ireland was achieved by a lower marriage age and a higher marriage rate.[35] By comparison, in southern Ireland, proportionately speaking, fewer women were having more babies and at a later stage in their life cycle.[36] Thus similar birth rates masked varying marital fertility profiles in the two states. In 1950, for example, the rate of children under 5 years of age per 100 married women (aged 15–44 years) was 122 in the Republic of Ireland, while it was only 91 in Northern Ireland and 61 for England and Wales.[37] The Republic of Ireland was therefore the true outlier with the North of Ireland finding itself somewhere in between the fertility patterns in the south of Ireland and those in England and Wales. Although much more research is required, particularly in relation to fertility practices in Northern Ireland, it is probable that religion, at least in part, underpinned these differences. In the south of Ireland over 90% of the population was Catholic in a state that prohibited birth control. In Northern Ireland the religious landscape was more varied with a third of the population belonging to the Catholic faith and almost two-thirds of the population affiliating with one of the Protestant Churches. Birth control was never explicitly banned in Northern Ireland, but nor did it become socially acceptable until the late 1960s and even then its reach was uneven. Indeed, there is significant evidence that faith, irrespective of religion, was of central importance in both parts of the country. For at least the first half of the twentieth century, the people on the island of Ireland shared a socially conservative outlook, bolstered by a traditional

Ó Gráda has noted that the difference in Catholic and Protestant family size in Ulster was marked by the early part of the century: Catholic fertility was two-thirds higher than that of Protestants in 1971. C. Ó Gráda, 'Did Ulster Catholics Always Have Larger Families?', *Irish Economic and Social History*, 12 (1985), pp. 79–80; D. Urquhart, 'Gender, Family and Sexuality in Ulster, 1800–2000', in L. Kennedy and P. Ollerenshaw (eds), *Ulster Since 1600* (Oxford: Oxford University Press, 2012), pp. 246–59.

[35] Urquhart, 'Marriage, Fertility and Sexuality in Ulster', pp. 246–59.

[36] J. Deeny, 'Perinatal Mortality in Ireland', *Irish Journal of Medical Science*, 30:8 (August 1955), p. 349.

[37] M. D. McCarthy, 'Some Family Facts in Ireland Today', *Christus Rex*, 5 (1951), pp. 46–64, p. 60.

sense of faith and family life, and a belief that sexuality should be governed by a strict moral code.

From the early 1920s the issue of maternal health was very much on the agenda in both states. The Irish Free State had a relatively high maternal mortality rate until the mid-1940s, often only rivalled by that of Northern Ireland and in both parts of the island maternal fertility remained unusually high until the 1970s and 1980s. Michael Solomons, an advocate of accessible birth control and founder of the Irish Family Planning movement in 1970s southern Ireland, noted: 'In the thirties the medical problems associated with unrestricted pregnancy, such as high blood pressure and anaemia, were compounded by a paucity of antenatal care, a general lack of education and poor nutrition. Mothers and their babies suffered. Ultimately many died'.[38] Solomons's father, Bethel Solomons had been Master of the Rotunda Protestant maternity hospital in Dublin between 1926 and 1933.[39] In 1934 he published an article in *The Lancet* in which he sought to explode the myth that 'in childbirth practice makes perfect', arguing that 'from the fifth pregnancy the rate of mortality is over average by an amount which increases steadily and speedily until in women bearing their tenth child or more the mortality is five times as high as for all women bearing children'.[40] He coined the phrase 'dangerous multipara' to describe these mothers. Irish mothers were inspiring a new lexicon to describe the danger that multiple pregnancies posed to them.[41] Thus, from very early on in the debate about women's reproductive health there were potent fears that the issue of women's health could provide grounds for contraception and abortion that might trump moral absolutism.[42]

[38] M. Solomons, *Pro Life? The Irish Question* (Dublin: Lilliput Press, 1992), p. 6.

[39] Bethel Solomons was born into a prominent Jewish family and was the first Jew to hold the position as Master of the Rotunda Hospital. William Murphy, 'Solomons, Bethel Albert Herbert', J. McGuire and J. Quinn (eds), *Dictionary of Irish Biography*, (Cambridge: Cambridge University Press, 2009), http://dib.cambridge.org.ucd.idm.oclc.org/viewReadPage.do?articleId=a8187.

[40] B. Solomons, 'The Dangerous Multipara', *Lancet* (7 July 1934), pp. 8–11.

[41] Ibid.

[42] S. McAvoy, '"A Perpetual Nightmare": Women, Fertility Control, the Irish State, and the 1935 Ban on Contraceptives', in M. H. Preston and M. Ó hÓgartaigh (eds), *Gender and Medicine in Ireland, 1700–1950* (New York: Syracuse University Press, 2012), pp. 189–202; Earner-Byrne, *Mother and Child*, pp. 34–58.

A 1922 article, in the Catholic periodical the *Irish Ecclesiastical Record*, argued that the case for either birth control or abortion on the grounds of saving the mother's life was 'an excuse in law'.[43] Rev. Vincent McNabb's speech of the following year given to the Catholic organisation of doctors, the Irish Guild of St. Luke, SS Cosmas and Damien, clearly outlined the Catholic medical perspective on birth control[44]:

> No doctor has the right to say to a married couple: 'You ought not to have any children at all; or if at all, then, only after a long interval.' All that may be said is a bare statement of the medical fact, in such words as: 'In my opinion, if you have another pregnancy at any time, or soon, you will die, or be ill, or risk the life of the child etc., etc.'[45]

In the same year, T. E. Flynn cited one of the underlying reasons for fearing the widespread availability of birth control in Ireland, when he pinpointed the potential freedom it would provide for Irish women to reject the exigencies of patriotism: 'What is there to induce women to go through the difficulties inseparable from maternity if they accept the principles of Birth Control? Patriotism?... Such motives will hardly succeed where the fear of God fails'.[46] Whether overt, as in this case, or implicit, the connection between Ireland's position in relation to birth control and abortion is intimately connected with the status accorded to Irish women: women's health was secondary to a claim of moral superiority; the risks were understood and consciously disregarded.[47]

[43] Rev. D. Barry, 'Medical Ethics', *Irish Ecclesiastical Record*, 20 (August 1922), pp. 168–80 cited in S. McAvoy, 'Before Cadden: Abortion in Mid-Twentieth-Century Ireland', in D. Keogh, F. O'Shea, and C. Quinlan (eds), *The Lost Decade: Ireland in the 1950s* (Cork, 2004), pp. 147–63, p. 148.

[44] See Dublin Diocesan Archives [hereafter DDA], Byrne Papers Box One: Lay Organisations, Stafford Johnson to Archbishop Byrne, 31 November 1931. See also, the inaugural address delivered before the Guild of SS Luke, Cosmas and Damien, Dublin, 21 April 1932, 'The True Idea and Outlook of a Catholic Medical Guild' by Dr. J. Stafford Johnson reprinted from the *Catholic Medical Guardian*, July 1932.

[45] Cited in Catholic Truth Society, *The Problem of Undesirable Printed Matter* (1931), p. 11.

[46] T. E. Flynn, 'The Moral Argument Against Birth Control', *The Dublin Review*, 173:347 (October–December 1923), pp. 243–62.

[47] See McAvoy, 'Before Cadden: Abortion in Mid-Twentieth-Century Ireland'.

For much of the twentieth century the only option available to Irish couples, if they wished to space or limit their families, was coitus interruptus (withdrawal) or abstinence.[48] While natural family methods became possible in the 1930s with the discovery of the 'safe period', Mary E. Daly argues that southern Ireland was particularly slow to embrace these methods.[49] Nonetheless, there is some evidence that information relating to these methods was circulating among the middling ranks of Irish society. In 1937, Professor of Economics, John Busteed, claimed that: 'during the past two years a remarkable distribution of the literature and knowledge of the subject has been quietly proceeding among the Irish middle classes'.[50] Yet he conceded that this would only happen if there was 'nothing immoral in the continence' and if 'facilities for the spread of the knowledge exist and are permitted'.[51] In fact, there was a deliberate effort on the part of the Irish Catholic Church to deny couples the knowledge required to 'naturally' control their fertility. For example, in 1934 a priest wrote into the problem page of the *Irish Ecclesiastical Record* asking if it was 'permissible' to teach the flock about 'the so-called sterile period in women'. He was told that relatively few married people should have need or justification to use this method: 'That in itself should be ample reason why the knowledge of this system should not be spread indiscriminately'.[52] Revealing characteristic paternalism, he pointed out that married couples could not be trusted as it was 'too easy for people to persuade themselves that the medical or social or eugenic indications...are verified in their case. Accordingly, we find the moralists who have written on the subject practically unanimous in urging that instruction on these matters should be as far as possible individual'.[53] In 1952, another priest asked if a married

[48] Fisher notes this was the preferred method in Britain prior to the widespread use of the contraceptive pill. K. Fisher, *Birth Control, Sex, and Marriage in Britain 1918–1960* (Oxford: Oxford University Press, 2006), p. 113.

[49] M. E. Daly, 'Rhythm and Blues: Natural Family Planning in Ireland', Unpublished Paper Presented at Centre for the History of Medicine in Ireland, 6 February 2014. The safe period was also known as the Ogino and Knaus method.

[50] J. Busteed, 'The Problem of Population', *Statistical and Social Inquiry Society of Ireland*, 15 (1937), pp. 47–70, p. 62.

[51] Discussion following Busteed's paper, ibid., p. 68.

[52] Anon., Notes and Queries: 'Diffusion of Knowledge Regarding the Sterile Period', *Irish Ecclesiastical Record*, 43 (1934), pp. 414–18, p. 417.

[53] Ibid., pp. 414–18.

couple with one or two children could be provided with this information; he was told that this would be 'imprudent and unlawful'.[54] He was also informed that it was not his job to advise people about 'fecundity', which was a curious response. Indeed, as Daly notes, 'most of the enforcement of Church teaching on contraception and large families was conducted in the confessional'.[55] This censorship of information, either in an informal way in the confessional or legally through the apparatus of the state, is a recurring theme in the Irish abortion journey. Information was power.

Such moral zeal resulted in landmark pieces of legislation in the Irish state, which remained in place until the 1970s and 1980s: the de facto absolute prohibition on divorce (1925), later enshrined in the Irish Constitution (1937) and the banning of information relating to birth control and abortion (1929).[56] In the interwar period, states like France and Italy introduced similar restrictions on birth control although the rationale was driven by pronatalism and fascism respectively. The 1930s saw renewed efforts in independent Ireland to ensure that the sale and use of birth control devices was also criminalised. While discussing the comprehensive ban on birth control in 1931, the Committee on the Criminal Law Amendment Act (1880–1885) and Juvenile Prostitution (popularly known as the Carrigan Committee), considered the idea of allowing doctors to prescribe birth control for women whose health was jeopardised by pregnancy, but the Criminal Law Amendment Act, 1935 introduced a complete ban on contraception with no exceptions.[57] Clearly, an informed decision had been made to safeguard morality over maternal health.

[54] Cited in Daly, 'Rhythm and Blues Natural Family Planning in Ireland'.

[55] Ibid.

[56] L. Earner-Byrne, 'Reinforcing the Family: The Role of Gender, Morality and Sexuality in Irish Welfare Policy, 1922–1944', *The History of the Family*, 13 (2008), pp. 360–96; L. Earner-Byrne, 'Moral Prescription: The Irish Medical Profession, the Roman Catholic Church and the Prohibition of Birth Control in Twentieth-Century Ireland', in C. Cox and M. Luddy (eds), *Cultures of Care in Irish Medical History, 1750–1970* (London: Palgrave Macmillan, 2010), pp. 207–28; C. Beaumont, 'Gender, Citizenship and the State in Ireland, 1922–1990', in S. Brewster, V. Crossman, F. Becket, and D. Alderson (eds), *Ireland in Proximity: History, Gender, and Space* (London: Routledge, 1999), pp. 94–108.

[57] See http://www.irishstatutebook.ie/eli/1935/act/6/section/17/enacted/en/html#sec17.

While, as noted, birth control was never criminalised in Northern Ireland, the general social ambivalence towards it is indicated by the fact that when the first Marie Stopes family planning clinic opened in Belfast in 1936, it met with antipathy and resistance. Although a Northern Irish Society for Constructive Birth Control [hereafter NISCBC] had been in existence since 1930, Stopes faced opposition and it 'took courage to be publicly associated with this cause'.[58] In continual deficit, the clinic made an unsuccessful approach to Belfast corporation for £100 towards its work in 1937.[59] It closed a decade later, after advising an estimated 3000–4000 women.[60] Its demise was in consequence of a lack of political and clerical support, particularly from the Catholic Church, but it laid the foundations for institutional family planning in Northern Ireland and confirmed a demand among some women (and, presumably men) to both limit and space births.[61]

Indeed, campaigners for birth control, many of them women, continued to give regular talks on the subject in Northern Ireland throughout the 1930s and 1940s. One woman, who was a senior member of the NISCBC, recalled of one such talk she gave in November 1940 to the Co-operative Women's Guild:

> Response to my talk much as usual – older women (in the majority) inclined to repeat they had eight (or ten or twelve) children and were none the worse for it. One woman (60ish) enquired 'doesn't all this bother with birth control make you neurotic?'...Younger women are more receptive, although shy of asking questions in front of people.[62]

[58] G. Jones, 'Marie Stopes in Ireland. The Mothers' Clinic in Belfast, 1936–1947', *Social History of Medicine*, 5:2 (1992), pp. 161, 263.

[59] The corporation claimed that it lacked the power to grant to monies requested. Minute book of Belfast Corporation Maternity and Child Welfare Committee, 1925–1940, 10 September 1937, Public Record Office of Northern Ireland [hereafter PRONI], LA/28/9/AD/2.

[60] Figures from Jones, 'Marie Stopes', p. 271.

[61] L. McCormick, '"The Scarlet Woman in Person": The Establishment of a Family Planning Service in Northern Ireland, 1950–1974', *Social History of Medicine*, 21:2 (2008), pp. 345–60, p. 347.

[62] Cited in M. Muldowney, 'Woman in Wartime: The Mass-Observation Diary of Moya Woodside', *The Irish Review*, 42 (Summer 2010), pp. 58–71, p. 63.

There is therefore some evidence of a generational divide in Northern Ireland on the issue of fertility control by the 1940s. While some older women were defensive, younger women were generally open to a different way of living, to a life in which they controlled their fertility rather than it controlling them. Some women had also evidently absorbed elements of the wider medical and popular debate that attempted to argue that birth control was harmful to women rendering them neurotic. This astute campaigner gave this short shrift: 'I told her how it soon became as automatic as your dentures, which amused the others greatly'. However, as Mary Muldowney observed, the subject of birth control was so fraught in Northern Ireland, that even this well-connected campaigner had to import her own supplies from Britain by mail order.[63] This is further evidence that although never criminalised, birth control was not socially acceptable for many women in Northern Ireland, who in practical terms found themselves in a similar position to their southern counterparts: birth control was simply beyond the moral pale or literal reach of many.

'Hard Cases' and Moral Absolutism

During the 1920s and 1930s growing fears concerning the impact of uncontrolled fertility on women's health resulted in a partial liberalisation of views in relation to birth control outside of independent Ireland.[64] For example, in 1930 the international Anglican Communion, of which the Church of Ireland was a member, accepted birth control within marriage for 'hard cases', referring in particular to a mother's exhaustion or family circumstances.[65] This decision prompted the Irish Catholic hierarchy, encouraged by zealous sections of the laity, to urge

[63] Ibid., p. 64.

[64] L. Earner-Byrne, 'Twixt God and Geography: The Development of Maternity Services in Twentieth-Century Ireland', in J. Greenless and L. Bryder (eds), *Western Maternity and Medicine, 1880–1990* (London: Pickering & Chatto, 2013), pp. 108–9. See also, S. Paŝeta, 'Censorship and Its Critics in the Free State, 1922–1932', *Past and Present*, 181 (2003), pp. 193–218.

[65] McAvoy, 'Before Cadden: Abortion in Mid-Twentieth-Century Ireland', p. 150. It should be noted that the Anglican communion was still morally opposed to birth control in any other circumstances. For a sense of the reluctance with which this slight relaxation of the ban on birth control in all circumstances engendered see, Bishop of Oxford, C. Gore, *Lambeth on Contraceptives* (London: Mowbray, 1930).

that the state prohibit Protestant doctors from serving as dispensary doctors (the medical service available for the poor) due to fears of any liberalising tendencies that might lead to abortion.[66] A memorandum prepared for government ministers even penned the option of criminalising therapeutic abortions which were performed to save a woman's life.[67] As Sandra McAvoy concludes: 'That such a possibility could even be pencilled…reflected the low status accorded to women in Irish society'.[68] However, the papal encyclical *Casti Connubii*, 'On Christian Marriage', issued in December 1930, had already effectively made this case by arguing that the idea that a mother's health offered morally acceptable grounds for the use of birth control was 'shameful' and 'false'.[69] In 1931, Rev. P. O'Neill claimed that the issue at the heart of the papal encyclical was the recognition of the true order of the family.[70] Thus, while the Church recognised the potential dangers that pregnancy might pose to a sick mother, the principle remained unaltered: 'the relation of the act [sex] to its primary end [of procreation] could not be disturbed'.[71] Contraception could not be tolerated on health grounds as morality was absolute.

In the early 1930s, the League of Nations was drawing up a maternal welfare report which warned that women who suffered from conditions such as heart disease, tuberculosis or nephritis should be advised not to get pregnant and be provided with 'anti-conception' advice.[72] The Catholic medical organisation, the Irish Guild of SS Luke, Cosmas and Damien, brought this to the attention of the Irish government, which resulted in the latter lobbying to have the wording changed. The League of Nations responded that it was not advocating the 'indiscriminate use of contraception', but merely wished to ensure that women were not 'called upon to sacrifice their lives'. The Irish government insisted that

[66] Rev. M. P. Cleary, 'The Church of Ireland and Birth Control', *Irish Ecclesiastical Record*, 38 (December 1931), pp. 622–29.

[67] Undated in Department of Justice memo., NAI, Department of Taoiseach, S2547B cited in McAvoy, 'Before Cadden: Abortion in Mid-Twentieth-Century Ireland', p. 149.

[68] McAvoy, 'Before Cadden: Abortion in Mid-Twentieth-Century Ireland', p. 149.

[69] See A. Fremantle, *The Papal Encyclicals in Their Historical Context* (New York: The New American Library, 1956), p. 239.

[70] Rev P. O'Neill, 'Casti Connubii', *Irish Ecclesiastical Record*, 37 (1931), p. 232.

[71] Ibid., p. 233.

[72] Nephritis is an inflammation of the kidneys.

while such women should be made aware of the dangers, they should not be provided with advice on avoiding pregnancy.[73] Following the Irish intervention, the League of Nations' handbook read: 'It is necessary further that the steps to be taken to avoid this should be explained to the husband and wife by a doctor, either privately or at a health centre, due account being taken of the individual's religious beliefs and moral principles, as well as of national legislation'.[74] The Irish state hailed this a victory. However, such a claim needs to be placed in the context of Ireland's high tuberculosis rates—a condition that, when combined with pregnancy, endangered women's lives.[75]

The Politics of Motherhood

Northern Ireland's maternal mortality rate was a perennial cause for concern throughout the interwar period; it was the highest in the UK in the 1920s.[76] In 1928, Northern Ireland Minister of Home Affairs, Richard Dawson Bates established a committee to examine the state's health provision.[77] Without the necessary finance to implement its recommendations, even though the need was pressing 'especially…with regard to maternity and child services', no change was forthcoming.[78] The report of the 1936 Committee of Enquiry into Maternal Health and Morbidity in Northern Ireland was also withheld from public scrutiny due to similar monetary concerns until 1943.[79] However, some members of the Northern Irish medical profession sensed how the official outlook in Britain was changing over the course of World War II, towards a belief that health care should be nationalised and free at the point of

[73] Extract from Coyne's report: Confidential statement re. section on contraception, issued by the League of Nations, c. 1932, NAI, Dept. of Health, B130/59.

[74] *Report of the Council on the Work of the Nineteenth Session of the Committee*, 15 October 1932, NAI, Dept. of Health, B130/59.

[75] G. Jones, *Captain of All These Men of Death: The History of Tuberculosis in Nineteenth and Twentieth Century Ireland* (Amsterdam and New York: Rodopi, 2001).

[76] J. F. O'Sullivan, 'The History of Obstetrics in Northern Ireland, 1921–1992', *Ulster Medical Journal*, 70:2 (November 2001), pp. 95–101, p. 95.

[77] The office of a dedicated Minister of Health was introduced to Northern Ireland in 1944.

[78] O'Sullivan, 'The History of Obstetrics', p. 96.

[79] The Northern Irish rate of maternal mortality was 7.3 per 1000 live births, in comparison to a rate of 4.9 in England and Wales at this juncture (ibid.).

entry for patients. Indeed, addressing his medical colleagues in Belfast in 1943, C. H. G. Macafee predicted: 'If my judgement is correct, the practice of obstetrics will become, in part at any rate, a state service'.[80] While Macafee's vision proved prescient, the process would be far from smooth in Northern Ireland, due in part to financial and religious concerns, particularly for Catholic hospitals.

The writings of Belfast woman Moya Woodside revealed some of the potential religious obstacles to a state-run maternity service. In March 1940, she began writing a diary on everyday life in the city for the Mass-Observation organisation in Britain. A member of the Protestant middle-class and Honorary Chairman of the Society for Constructive Birth Control Northern Ireland, her insights into life in the city during the war poignantly reveal the impact of poverty.[81] She also illuminated the complexity of reproductive politics in Northern Ireland which were imbued with religious tensions and sensibilities. Woodside, very much a product of her class and upbringing, clearly attempted to 'be tolerant', but found bearing witness to what she regarded as the reproductive slavery of Catholic women extremely challenging to her own maternalistic instincts. On 10 March 1940, she recorded the following encounter:

> At welfare office this morning, interviewed a woman who said she was 28, but looked to be 40 – toothless, haggard, undernourished, thin lank hair. She was the mother of 8 *living* children, 3 of them tubercular, was suspected of TB herself and her husband, of course, long-term unemployed. Roman Catholic. I try not to be intolerant, but a religion which turns women into reproductive machines, regardless of the effect on health or happiness, is brutal and inhumane… And there are thousands like her in this city alone.[82]

Here was a veteran birth control campaigner confronted with the realities of life for the poorest Catholics in her city. While she would instinctively have liked to free this woman from her womb, she was aware of the socio-political reasons why that might have been perceived as an act

[80] C. G. H. Macafee, 'Medical Students and the Teaching of Midwifery', *Ulster Medical Journal*, 1:12 (1943), pp. 24–40, p. 38.

[81] For a real sense of the depth of this poverty outside the cities, see, J. M. Mogey, *Rural Life in Northern Ireland* (Oxford: Oxford University Press, 1947).

[82] Muldowney, 'Woman in Wartime: The Mass-Observation Diary of Moya Woodside', p. 62.

of intolerance or disrespect.[83] In later years she reflected on the difficulties of integrating birth control as part of medical care prior to the National Health Service [hereafter NHS]:

> a few medical men...were prepared to come out publicly in support of a birth control clinic, although they might privately agree with the need. It is sometimes forgotten that consultants in those pre-NHS days, did their own hospital work on a voluntary basis, and relied for their living on fees from patients sent to them privately by G.P.s. My late husband, a surgeon, did become a sponsor, but he thought that if the Clinic brochure was widely circulated, he would never get any more patients from Roman Catholic G.P.s.[84]

Only the creation of the NHS, operative in Northern Ireland from 1948, removed the financial insecurity which dictated healthcare provision in the province, but it could not transform the culture of conservatism that pertained towards birth control and women's reproductive health. This ultimately meant that there was minimal counselling or support available for those experiencing an unplanned pregnancy.[85] However, the fact that Northern Irish mothers were entitled to a free healthcare service was a revolutionary development enabling even the poorest to access care. Its reach was not, however, absolute as the Catholic Mater Infirmorium Hospital in Belfast, stayed outside of the NHS until 1972.[86] Despite this, as Peter Martin has noted, the NHS was 'probably the most successful element of the welfare state in Northern Ireland' and 'was popular with both communities and was kept out of the political affray'.[87]

[83]Muldowney points out that in Woodside's later career in America, she wrote approvingly of the eugenic sterilization programme of the government of North Carolina, which raises questions about some of her motivations. Indeed, Catholics in Ireland often used the association of the birth control movement with eugenics as another reason to discredit contraception (ibid.).

[84]Letter from M. Woodside to L. A. Hall, Wellcome Institute of the History of Medicine, London, 6 August 1981. Cited in Muldowney, 'Woman in Wartime: The Mass-Observation Diary of Moya Woodside', p. 63.

[85]This was the result of the Health Service (NI) Act, 1946. O'Sullivan, 'The History of Obstetrics in Northern Ireland', p. 95.

[86]P. Martin, 'Social Policy and Social Change Since 1914', in Kennedy and Ollerenshaw (eds), *Ulster Since 1600*, pp. 308–23, p. 315.

[87]Ibid., p. 316. The reference here to two communities is to those who wished to see a united Ireland (nationalist and usually Catholic) and those who supported Northern Ireland's place with the United Kingdom (unionists and usually Protestant).

While the provisions of the NHS were being embedded in Northern Ireland, the mother-and-child controversy in the Republic of Ireland propelled the issue of maternity and church–state relations to centre-stage in the early 1950s. The controversy centred on a scheme to introduce free maternity care for all women and children up to sixteen years of age. The Catholic hierarchy and the Irish Medical Association [IMA] both vehemently opposed it as the 'socialisation of motherhood'.[88] The nub of the issue was who would control and profit from maternity care in Ireland. Ultimately, the scheme failed, and the government fell due to behind the scene machinations involving the Catholic hierarchy, the IMA and the government. No one came away from the debacle well: the government failed to support its own policy initiative, party politics was shamelessly exercised in the Irish parliament, the IMA prioritised its revenue anxieties over healthcare reform and the Catholic hierarchy appeared more fearful of state power and that women may be informed how to control their fertility, than about ensuring safety in childbirth and equitable access to health care.

Letters poured into Irish newspapers criticising the Catholic Church's stance. Although most opted for anonymity, Dr. G. W. Roberts, writing from North Wales, described the comprehensive health care mothers received in Wales and articulated genuine confusion at what had happened in the Republic of Ireland: 'the whole scheme has been sabotaged…by the Hierarchy on very flimsy – if not on non-existent – grounds…The mothers and children have been deprived of their right to expert medical care and attention and in many cases to their right even to life'.[89] Crucially, this controversy revealed the potential for the issue of maternity to generate deep ideological divides. It also illuminated where power lay in Irish society. Many 1950 contemporaries believed that the Catholic Church had been on the wrong side of the mother-and-child debate and the controversy came to be seen as a precursor to the deeper estrangement from the church that would later occur.[90] In 1953, a

[88]The best account remains E. McKee, 'Church-State Relations and the Development of Irish Health Policy: The Mother-and-Child Scheme, 1944–1953', *Irish Historical Studies*, 25:98 (1986), pp. 159–94.

[89]*Irish Times*, 20 April 1951 cited in R. Guyett-Nicholson, 'Yours etc.—Public Perceptions of the Mother and Child Scheme' (Unpublished MA Paper, UCD, 2018).

[90]This was, in part, due to the 1968 papal encyclical *Humanae Vitae* which is discussed in Chapter 4.

considerably watered-down health act was introduced which provided free maternity services for mothers in lower and middle-income groups and their infants up to six weeks.[91]

Conclusion

The history of Ireland's export of abortion lies therefore in an often-ecumenical moral orthodoxy. As the number of Irish Catholic doctors who were instrumental in getting the Irish State to lobby against the League of Nations' endorsement of birth control on health grounds revealed, the health needs of women were continuously and consciously sidelined. As late as 1956 some doctors were cautioning that women should never be told a pregnancy could kill them in case this led to a request for a termination.[92] As Betty Hilliard notes, 'women relied on a combination of luck, natural methods and their partner's co-operation to curtail the number of their pregnancies'.[93] The 'uncertainty of these strategies' overshadowed many marriages and meant that for Irish women sex was often 'beset with fears' as each month brought a potential pregnancy.[94]

Many Irish women found ways to navigate the restrictive moral climate pertaining on the island of Ireland, but the solutions were often outside the state and at significant personal and financial cost. The irony

[91] Health Act, 1935. For full details see, http://www.irishstatutebook.ie/eli/1953/act/26/enacted/en/html. For discussion of its historical relevance to women's health care see, Earner-Byrne, *Mother and Child*, pp. 163–68.

[92] See A. P. Barry, D. Meagher, and E. O'Dwyer, 'Heart Disease in Pregnancy', *Journal of the Irish Medical Association*, 38 (1956), pp. 82–83 cited in C. Clear, *Women of the House: Women's Household Work in Ireland, 1926–1961* (Dublin: Irish Academic Press, 2000), p. 123. There is also the history of symphysiotomy, a practice continued in Ireland well into the 1980s by Catholic doctors as an alternative to caesarean sections.

[93] B. Hilliard, 'Motherhood, Sexuality and the Catholic Church', in P. Kennedy (ed.), *Motherhood in Ireland* (Cork: Mercier Press, 2000), p. 144; See Fisher's work on the reality of these intimate negotiations in Britain for the same period. K. Fisher, '"She Was Quite Satisfied with the Arrangements I Made": Gender and Birth Control in Britain 1920–1950', *Past and Present*, 169 (2000), pp. 161–93. The stories recorded in K. Kearns, *Dublin Tenement Life: An Oral History* (Dublin: Gill and MacMillan, 1994) repeatedly testify to lack of negotiation in relation to sexual matters—mothers in general did not perceive that they had an option with regard to sexual intercourse and when, or how often, it occurred.

[94] Hilliard, 'Motherhood, Sexuality and the Catholic Church', p. 145.

was not lost on a few: independent Ireland could never have maintained its illusion of moral superiority without the backdoor solutions provided by Britain. The Northern Irish state, with conservatism embedded and embraced by many Catholics and Protestants, in fact mirrored many of the moral anxieties seen across the border. Thus, the prenatal export of women from both independent and Northern Ireland established the foundations of dealing with reproductive issues outside of both states. It is also possible to identify a narrative of moral fundamentalism in both jurisdictions, which enabled the evasion of more complex ethical and medical issues until at least the 1970s and, arguably, to the present day. At the heart of this was a desire to control the flow of information to ensure that women were not fully aware of the health implications of repeated pregnancies in case that might encourage abortion. This was underpinned by an acknowledgment that in prioritising morality over medicine some women would die.

CHAPTER 3

Legality and Irish Abortion, 1920s–1960s

Abstract Since the foundation of both states on the island of Ireland women have had to face the risks inherent in pregnancy and navigate moral, legal and social controls. The issue of fertility control was driven underground in Ireland until the 1960s which resulted in the illegal importation of contraceptives in independent Ireland and backstreet abortions and prosecutions against those who broke the law in both jurisdictions. This chapter explores circumstances under which legal and illegal abortions were carried out on the island of Ireland prior to 1967. It also examines the consequences of the restrictive abortion regime for Irish women.

Keywords Abortionists · Underground · Therapeutic abortion · Criminal abortion · Maternal health · Fertility

For much of the twentieth century, women on the island of Ireland had to face the risks inherent in pregnancy and navigate moral, legal and social controls: birth control was prohibited in the south of Ireland and inaccessible to many in the North and abortion remained illegal in both jurisdictions. The 1861 Offences Against the Person Act, which criminalised a pregnant woman who tried to procure an abortion and anyone who assisted her in that endeavour, continued to govern abortion law in Ireland after the foundation of both states. While the UK's Infant

L. Earner-Byrne and D. Urquhart, *The Irish Abortion Journey, 1920–2018*, Genders and Sexualities in History,
https://doi.org/10.1007/978-3-030-03855-7_3

Life (Protection) Act, 1929 permitted abortions to save the life of the mother, this was not enacted in Northern Ireland. Thus there was no provision in law in either jurisdiction in Ireland for abortions to save a mother's life, however, there is evidence that these abortions did occur. Thus this chapter examines the medical profession's role in creating a place in medical practice for abortions, which were deemed permissible on the grounds of risk to the mother's life.[1] The medical profession in both parts of the island effectively worked out what constituted grounds for therapeutic abortions throughout the 1920s and 1930s, developing best practice covered implicitly, if not legally, by the idea of 'good faith' which governed all medical practice. While only Northern Ireland was directly impacted by developing case law in the UK, southern Ireland was clearly aware of these trends, in particular, arguments emerging in the 1930s regarding the distinctions between abortion on the grounds of the maternal threat to life *or* health. This chapter also considers the evidence relating to 'backstreet' abortions, which occurred outside the clinical environment. It explores the prosecutions against those who broke the law regarding abortion and the fate of the pregnant women at the centre of this often-hidden aspect of abortion history.[2] Some cases, like that of the abortionist Nurse Cadden in the Republic of Ireland in the mid-1950s, attracted a significant amount of public attention due to the death of the pregnant women involved.[3] This helped to embed in the Irish consciousness the idea that abortion was synonymous with danger and criminality. However, the majority of abortions probably went undetected

[1]Mollie Dunsmuir, 'Abortion: Constitutional and Legal Developments', 18 August 1998, http://www.publications.gc.ca/Collection-R/LoPBdP/CIR/8910-e.htm, accessed 4 November 2018.

[2]See P. Conroy, 'Maternity Confined—The Struggle for Fertility Control', in P. Kennedy (ed.), *Motherhood in Ireland* (Cork: Mercier Press, 2000), p. 131; Kennedy noted that the subject was rarely mentioned in Ireland but that the case of Nurse Cadden, a backstreet abortionist, brought the issue to public attention in the 1950s. Nurse Cadden became in popular imagination and media coverage the 'personification of evil'. F. Kennedy, *Cottage to Crèche: Family Change in Ireland* (Dublin: The Institute of Public Administration, 2001), p. 39.

[3]For a review of the case of Nurse Cadden see NAI, Dept. of Taoiseach, S16116. McAvoy, 'Before Cadden: Abortion in Mid-Twentieth-Century Ireland', pp. 147–63; Conroy, 'Maternity Confined', p. 127. See also McAvoy, 'Its Effect on Public Morality Is Vicious in the Extreme', pp. 35–52.

and, in consequence, few asked why these women sought terminations or what impact continuing with pregnancies might have on their health.

Therapeutic Abortions

In the early decades of the twentieth century many women were not aware that they had no say in whether or not they could have an abortion. Medical practitioners in both the north and south of Ireland reported that they were often asked to perform abortions by pregnant women, who were then shocked to discover this was not legally possible. Dr. Thomas Holmes, head of the Jubilee Maternity Hospital in Belfast from 1926 to 1949, noted that between 800 and 1000 women came to the hospital each year seeking abortions and women made similar requests at the city's Marie Stopes' clinic and the Church of Ireland's Midnight Mission.[4] In the south of Ireland, Bethel Solomons also alluded to the fact that women frequently came to Dublin's Rotunda maternity hospital requesting abortions. For example, in his 1929 revision of the main obstetric textbook used at the maternity hospital, he advised: 'It is well to warn the young practitioner that he should learn well the ethics of abortion. He will get frequent offers to induce him to empty the uterus, and he must remember that he risks reputation and liberty by acceptance of any of them'.[5] It seemed that women frequently implored their doctors to help them secure an abortion, but Solomons warned not only of the ethical risks of complying with these requests, but of the legal possibility of 'the extreme penalty as the professional abortionist'. Solomons was, nevertheless, cognisant of the real risks to some women's health posed by pregnancy. He echoed the very phrase Irish Catholic doctors advocated using with such patients; hence the young practitioner was told: 'A woman who is tubercular should

[4] Neither Stopes' Mothers' Clinic or the Midnight Mission in Belfast provided advice on abortion. Founded in the nineteenth century, the Midnight Mission ran a home for prostitutes and unmarried mothers as well as a maternity home. It also provided antenatal visits, boarding out and adoption services. It changed its name to Malone Place Maternity and Rescue Home in 1944. Lack of financial support from the local authority led the Midnight Mission to close in 1949. For Irish letters to Marie Stopes see, C. Ó Gráda, *Ireland: A New Economic History* (Oxford: Oxford University Press, 1995), pp. 218–25.

[5] B. Solomons (ed.), *Tweedy's Practical Obstetrics* (Oxford and London: Oxford Medical Publications, 6th ed., 1929), p. 222. Solomons described this book as embodying 'The Principles and Methods of Treatment at Present Practised at the Rotunda Hospital'.

be advised not to marry: if she marries, she should be advised not to become pregnant…'.[6] Similarly, 'A woman with cardiac disease should be advised not to marry if she has presented symptoms of heart failure such as dyspnoea [laboured breathing], cyanosis [discolouration of the skin due to an increase in deoxygenated haemoglobin levels], haemoptysis [the coughing of blood], dropsy [swelling of soft tissue due to excess water] …'.[7] His medical opinion of a tubercular woman's prospects was bleak: 'During pregnancy she may improve a little in her general health, but she becomes very ill after the child is born, and death often ensues'.[8] Where he deviated from his Catholic counterparts was in his conclusion that this condition provided the grounds for induction in the first three months of pregnancy, in effect a therapeutic abortion. In addition, he urged, women with 'decompensated heart disease…should not be allowed to go through the strain of pregnancy' and if rest and medical treatment did not result in a change in her condition within seven to ten days 'the pregnancy should be terminated'.[9]

Thus, in the south of Ireland, therapeutic abortions were clearly occurring when the life of the mother was at risk, but their condition had to be acute and death must be imminent, always presenting the risk of waiting too long and both mother and baby dying as a consequence. Indeed, several textbooks written by various Masters of the Rotunda hospital throughout the 1920s and 1930s outlined situations in which therapeutic abortions *should* be carried out.[10] Gibbon Fitzgibbon's 1937 *Obstetrics*, for example, stated unambiguously that in cases of cardiac failure in the early stages of pregnancy, it was 'best…to terminate the pregnancy' and the 'termination of pregnancy may be indicated at any time on behalf of the mother, or in the last few weeks of pregnancy on

[6] Ibid., p. 317.

[7] Ibid.

[8] Ibid.

[9] Ibid., p. 318.

[10] The authors were: Gibbon Fitzgibbon, Church of Ireland; Ninian Falkiner, Unitarian; Bethel Solomons, Jewish; O'Donel Brown, Church of Ireland. The texts were: O'Donel Browne, *A Manual of Practical Obstetrics* (Bristol: John Wright, 1936); B. Solomons and N. M. Falkiner, *Tweedy's Practical Obstetrics* (Oxford and London: Oxford Medical Publications, 7th ed., 1937); G. Fitzgibbon, *Obstetrics* (Dublin: Browne and Nolan, 1937). For a discussion of these texts see, Peter Morris, 'The Statute Law on Abortion in Ireland', in Jennifer Schweppe (ed.), *The Unborn Child, Article 40.3.3 and Abortion in Ireland: Twenty-Five Years of Protection?* (Dublin: Liffey Press, 2008), pp. 277–300.

behalf of the infant'.[11] Fitzgibbon also claimed that in an unnamed Irish hospital therapeutic abortions had been performed in thirteen cases of hyperemesis gravidarum (acute morning sickness) in the previous three years.[12]

Nevertheless, Solomons made clear to the student reader that 'At present, social, economic, and eugenic reasons cannot be cited as reasons' for terminating a pregnancy.[13] He was also critical of 'criminal abortions' and believed that doctors should be alert to the possibility that such cases may come their way:

> If a woman consults a doctor, and he believes a criminal abortion has been attempted, he should immediately call in a consultant. He should treat the case and endeavour to save the woman's life. If he is sure of his facts, and he thinks it advisable, the police should be acquainted, but this step should be taken only after prolonged consideration.[14]

While he highlighted that the doctor–patient relationship should protect a woman from prosecution, for instance, if the consultant was sure it was a case of criminal abortion, his first duty was to save the woman, but then he must seriously consider whether to involve the police. Solomons was evidently cautious about advocating the doctor as moral gatekeeper, but not completely adverse to the notion either. Furthermore, he clearly saw 'criminal abortions' as presenting a serious risk to women's health:

> Criminal abortion is usually a synonymous term with septic abortion, because it is only discovered when severe sepsis arises. It is most usually caused by rupture of the uterus with a dirty catheter or other instrument. The practitioner must take great care how he involves himself in a case of true criminal abortion: most of these cases are undertaken by unskilled and unscrupulous persons, and a lack of aseptic technique, together with severe traumatism of the uterus, may be sufficient to produce severe symptoms.[15]

[11] Fitzgibbon, *Obstetrics*, p. 381 cited in Morris, 'The Statute Law on Abortion in Ireland', p. 292; for other conditions that would warrant a termination, see pp. 423–26.

[12] Fitzgibbon, *Obstetrics*, p. 361.

[13] Ibid., p. 222.

[14] Solomons, *Tweedy's Practical Obstetrics*, p. 226.

[15] Ibid., p. 236.

Implicit in this was the acknowledgment that the risk to women's health was posed less by the abortion than the environment in which one must take place: it was not legally possible for a woman to have a safe abortion on request, so she had no choice but to resort to those willing to carry them out illegally outside the clinical environment. Although these abortionists were, of course, not always 'unscrupulous persons', women in need often had no way of judging until it was too late. Coupled with these risks, the woman who needed further medical attention after procuring such an abortion often encountered blinding prejudice that further increased her risks. For example, in Solomons's own hospital in 1932, a twenty-five-year-old woman was admitted after swallowing a large amount of abortificients. After three months of procrastination, hyperglycaemia [high blood sugar] was diagnosed and she was given a minor section. She died. Solomons frankly recorded the lethal impact of moral judgement: 'This woman might have been saved by an earlier minor section, but her desire for abortion rather cloaked the gravity of her case and probably warped judgment'.[16]

In Northern Ireland, there is also evidence to indicate that therapeutic abortions were performed in situations where the mother's life was in danger. It is interesting to note that at the same time as the Irish Free State government was negotiating with the League of Nations about whether or not pregnant women should be provided with birth control when their lives were at risk, doctors in Northern Ireland were grappling with similar problems. In 1932, S. L. Turkington, who had been a Tuberculosis Medical Officer and was working in Belfast's Royal Victoria Hospital, explained that women with pulmonary tuberculosis rarely fared well when pregnant: 'My own experience is that pregnancy is definitely very harmful to cases of early phthisis [wasting of the body]'. He pointed to medical opinion that advised an abortion should be performed prior to fifth month of pregnancy.[17] In 1936, H. I. McClure, then Assistant Surgeon at the Royal Maternity Hospital, Belfast explained, 'in patients where there is any degree of cardiac inefficiency in the early months, termination of the pregnancy must be considered'. In fact, he went so far

[16]'The Annual Report of the Rotunda', *Irish Journal of Medical Science*, 92 (August 1933), p. 334.

[17]S. I. Turkington, 'Problems of Phthisis', *Ulster Medical Journal* [Hereafter *UMJ*], 1:4 (1932), pp. 204–14, p. 210.

as to declare termination of pregnancy 'imperative if these cases fail to improve'. He also broached sterilization, a subject that was simply taboo in the south of Ireland, suggesting this was the best course of action for some of these patients. Revealingly, where the medics operating in the south of Ireland dealt with the subject of terminations with brevity, McClure went into considerable detail regarding how best they might be performed.[18]

Thomas S. S. Holmes of the Jubilee Hospital in Belfast also addressed the *Ulster Medical Society* in 1941 on the subject of abortion, conceding that it was an issue that had 'a certain suggestion of impropriety'.[19]

In a remarkably similar attitude to Solomons, Holmes described 'criminal abortion' as evidenced by the damage it caused to the female body as the professional abortionist used equipment to either pass 'a sound into the uterus, or injection of soap and water through the cervical canal': 'The criminal abortion, that is an induced one, is diagnosed by direct evidence of injury—lacerations, perforations, or foreign bodies in the cervix, or by definite history of operation, interference, or drug-taking'.[20] Holmes worried about how hard it was to secure a conviction in cases of abortion noting that 'acutely ill and afraid' women gave 'meticulous and convincing evidence', but often denied their story later when recovered. Even if women co-operated, in his experience, without 'several policemen and a couple of reputable doctors [who] are actual witnesses of the crime…conviction seems impossible'. For Holmes retribution was sometimes left to God, revealing the level of moral judgement and hostility towards abortionists. He therefore described it as 'poetic justice' when an abortionist inadvertently caused her own death:

> in the ordinary course of nature she missed a couple of periods – her age was the mid-forties. Just to make sure, she passed an instrument on herself, perforated her uterus, and died of an acute septicaemia. She was not pregnant. This time the mills of the Lord ground exceedingly small.[21]

[18] H. I. McClure, 'Heart Disease Complicating Pregnancy', *UMJ*, 5:4 (1936), pp. 234–40, p. 237.

[19] T. S. S. Holmes, 'The Incidence of Abortion at the Jubilee Hospital, Belfast', *UMJ*, 10:1 (April 1941), pp. 2–4.

[20] Ibid., p. 2.

[21] Ibid., p. 3.

However, as Mark Benson's detailed study of abortion in Northern Ireland between 1900 and 1968 suggests, there was significant sympathy for women who sought abortions and despite the 'societal rhetoric…there was no desire to punish everyone involved in this crime'.[22] There are a few intriguing whispers at the edges of these abortion stories. Holmes, for example, talks of 'a mid-wife, who was a known abortionist' and expressed surprise at how easily women would tell a 'kindly nurse' what they had done or had had done to themselves because they 'had no sense of wrong-doing in the matter'.[23] Holmes was also somewhat bemused that some Northern Irish women believed they had a right to an abortion upon request and were surprised when that 'request is not granted'. This indicates that women were ignorant of the illegality of abortion up to the 1940s; it is surely no coincidence that this timeframe coincides with the transition from home to hospital births, which occurred in Ireland between 1920s and 1940s. It is possible that the movement of childbirth to hospital denied women some abortion options more readily available when childbirth was overseen in a domestic setting by local handywomen (a term used to describe unqualified midwives). Indeed, Cara Delay notes how often handywomen, nurses, and midwives featured in court cases regarding criminal abortion in the south of Ireland, remarking that this role 'warrants further exploration'.[24] Furthermore, Holmes's pessimism and Solomons's hesitancy regarding convictions for criminal abortions implied that the medical profession—the people often with knowledge of such—were reluctant players in any courtroom drama. As Benson argues, although some doctors appeared in court, evidence given in many trials indicates that 'numerous medical professionals were providing a discreetly legal [abortion] service across Northern Ireland'.[25] In other words, the flexibility of acting in 'good faith' and

[22] M. T. S. Benson, 'The Provision of Abortion in Northern Ireland, 1900–1968' [Unpublished PhD thesis, Queen's University Belfast, 2017], p. 362.

[23] Holmes, 'The Incidence of Abortion at the Jubilee Hospital, Belfast', p. 2.

[24] C. Delay, 'Pills, Potions, and Purgatives: Women and Abortion Methods in Ireland, 1900–1950', *Women's History Review* (2018), pp. 1–22, p. 12.

[25] Benson, 'The Provision of Abortion in Northern Ireland', p. 281.

shielded by their medical qualifications, allowed doctors to perform abortions that might otherwise have been considered illegal, if performed by other people in different circumstances. That is not to suggest that these doctors did not consider their actions legitimate or to have been done genuinely in the spirit of 'good faith', but rather that the legal world was more likely to trust their judgement in ambiguous or unclear cases than that of women themselves or other abortion actors.[26]

While the 1861 Offences Against the Person Act remained in situ, the UK's Infant Life (Protection) Act, 1929 permitted abortions to save the life of the mother. Although not enacted in Northern Ireland, the act was central to the 1938 case of Aleck Bourne, a renowned London gynaecologist and obstetric surgeon, who was accused of 'procuring the miscarriage' of a 14-year-old girl. This case brought the question of therapeutic abortions centre stage. The girl in question had become pregnant as a result of rape and her father consented to her abortion due to concerns for her mental state. Although lambasted as an 'interference with motherhood' by the prosecution, Bourne was acquitted to loud applause in the courtroom.[27] This case had an important impact on medical and public opinion in Britain in relation to abortion. The English press rightly mused on its wide implications and expressed relief that it had given 'much-needed clarification of the legal provision' by bringing 'the law openly into line with medical and public opinion'.[28] The case was covered by the press in both jurisdictions in Ireland, but the lack of editorial comment was indicative of a wider malaise. Although the *Belfast News-letter* deemed it 'one of the most important trials in medico-legal history', it only reprinted coverage from a selection of English papers.[29] This classic distancing tactic was also apparent in the Northern Ireland parliament; it made no mention of the case. Likewise, at the time, the

[26] Benson offers a wonderfully nuanced discussion of this. Ibid., pp. 247–51.

[27] H. A. K. Morgan, Prosecution in the Bourne Case, 1938, *Belfast News-letter*, 2 July 1938.

[28] *News-Chronicle* cited in *Belfast News-Letter*, 20 July 1938.

[29] Extracts from the *Daily Telegraph*, *The Times* and the *News-Chronicle* were included. *Belfast News-letter*, 20 July 1938.

UMJ ignored both the case and its potential implications for medical practice in the UK. Despite Northern Ireland's best efforts to ignore the fact, the Bourne case made it legally permissible to abort when needed to save the patient's life and this definition was accepted as incorporating both physical ***and*** mental wellbeing. While abortion without restriction was not established by Bourne, Justice Macnaghten's summing up in this case had implications well beyond England:

> If...the life of a woman can be saved by performing an operation...and the doctor refuses to perform it on account of some religious opinion and the women dies, he would be in grave peril of being brought before this court on a charge of manslaughter by negligence.[30]

This ruling provided case law that placed the legal onus on a doctor to perform an abortion when necessary to save the mother's life, including against the threat of suicide, irrespective of the doctor's own moral position. Thus, the 1938 case clarified that: when assessing the risks a pregnancy posed to a woman's life, a doctor must consider her mental health ***and*** doctors were legally bound not just to refuse to perform illegal abortions, but also to perform legal abortions. The failure to perform a therapeutic abortion to save a woman's life could leave a doctor exposed to manslaughter charges.

In the south of Ireland, the Bourne case was also hailed as of 'great interest to the medical profession'. Interestingly, the southern press pointed out that many in England believed the abortion law was unsatisfactory and that Bourne had performed the abortion to 'ventilate the issue' and force reform.[31] When reporting Bourne's acquittal, the *Irish Times* quoted the judge regarding the complexity of differentiating between performing an abortion for the mother's life versus her health: 'I confess I have great difficulty in understanding what the discussion means. Life depends on health, and it may be that health is so gravely impaired that death results'. The judge was clearly arguing that the distinction between an abortion to save a mother's life as opposed to her health was a spurious one as the two—life and

[30] *Belfast News-Letter*, 20 July 1938. The term abortion was fastidiously avoided in the press coverage of this case and others.

[31] 'London Surgeon Sent for Trial', *Irish Times*, 2 July 1938.

health—were indistinguishable. As the *Irish Times* observed, the jury had been asked to consider if the doctor had acted in 'good faith…for the purposes of preserving the life of the mother' and it had ruled he had. In view of the distinction that would be drawn in the Republic of Ireland from 1983 between a mother's life and health, this was an early airing of the lines of argument holding sway in Britain.[32] While the Bourne case clearly had an impact on the thinking of key figures in the medical profession in Northern Ireland and likely accounted, at least in part, for the rise in the numbers of therapeutic abortions performed in Northern Irish hospitals, it is very difficult to ascertain its effect on doctors in the south of Ireland. The discussion of even therapeutic abortion became hugely constricted in the Irish Free State in the wake of the 1929 Censorship Act and the 1935 Criminal Law Amendment Act.[33]

Acts of Desperation

For countless women on the island of Ireland there were limited options when facing an unwanted pregnancy: infanticide; concealment of birth; the abandonment of a child; adoption, or an illegal abortion at home or in Britain. R. S. Rose, for example, notes that there were higher rates of infanticide and related crimes in the south of Ireland 'than any of the other areas investigated in the British Isles. …the evidence is… consistent with the supposition that unwanted Irish pregnancies have to a greater extent been historically more likely to end in post-natal fatalities than elsewhere in the British Isles'.[34] This is all the more striking as the Northern Irish rates of infanticide and concealment of birth ranked in 'a close second' place.[35] Cliona Rattigan's aptly entitled study of

[32] 'Surgeon Not Guilty', *Irish Times*, 20 July 1938.

[33] For an interesting account of the impact of the 1929 censorship act on public debate in the Irish Free State see, A. Keating, 'A Shot Across the Bows of Journalism in the Irish Free State', *History Ireland*, 20 (2012), https://www.historyireland.com/20th-century-contemporary-history/a-shot-across-the-bows-of-journalism-in-the-irish-free-state/.

[34] R. S. Rose, 'Induced Abortion in the Republic of Ireland', *British Journal of Criminology*, 18:3 (July 1978), pp. 253–54.

[35] Ibid., p. 253.

infanticide, '*What else could I do?*' (a question posed by a female defendant), evokes the desperation implicit in so many of the infanticides carried out by Irish women and their relatives.[36] Rattigan's study of over 300 infanticide cases tried in the higher courts in independent Ireland in the first half of the twentieth century confirms that women who committed such acts were not the 'girl murderers' conjured by contemporary media, but more often women who had reached the age of majority. Similar to abortion cases, quite a few of the women on trial had long-term relationships and expected to marry the fathers of their child.[37] While Rattigan provides examples of compassion, the most searing image is that of Irish women, pregnant or with newborns in-tow, wandering the Irish countryside, sleeping in fields, hiding in barns, literally frozen out of society, driven to the margins and, at times, the very edge of despair, to murder their infants.[38] Rattigan concludes that this evidence suggests that the focus of the courts was on the 'containment of women's sexuality' rather than the welfare of their infants.[39] This is supported by the fact that women convicted of infanticide or concealment of birth,[40] who had one out-of-wedlock pregnancy tended to be sentenced to a convent, mother-and-baby home or refuge, for moral reform. Women with several such pregnancies were sent to prison with hard labour, presumably because they were considered beyond redemption. Furthermore, some unmarried women convicted of concealment of birth were released if they agreed to marry the father, most likely because this was believed to render her under male control and respectable. All these social responses to unmarried mothers highlight how the issue was framed in moral rather than welfare terms.

Some Irish women were rendered so desperate by the desire to end a pregnancy that they attempted to self-abort by using pills, herbal remedies, douches, physical exercise, syringes and salt baths before

[36] C. Rattigan, *What Else Could I Do? Single Mothers and Infanticide, Ireland 1900–1950* (Dublin: Irish Academic Press, 2012).

[37] Ibid., p. 139.

[38] Ibid., pp. 54, 61.

[39] Ibid., p. 212.

[40] Many women were convicted of the lesser offence of 'concealment of birth', which was the failure to declare and register a birth.

seeking help from anyone else. Much of the historical research points to an array of methods that were evidently circulating in local female networks.[41] Of the thirty-three Northern Irish cases of illegal abortion heard in Belfast courts up to 1967, for instance, a third admitted to taking substances, often pills.[42] Five of these women died after attempting to use a syringe to abort, a practice which could cause shock, haemorrhage, embolism (blockage in a blood vessel), perforation of the uterus or sepsis.[43] All the main studies of abortion during this period confirm that 'word-of-mouth' was how Irish women became aware of both methods and abortionists.[44] Handywomen, other women who had abortions, sympathetic nurses or midwives were the characters that most often featured in these female networks. Women passed on advertisements they had found or methods they believed had worked previously for them. The pharmacist was also often consulted by the woman who wished to 'bring on her period' or her 'monthly curse'.[45] These conversations were often framed in euphemistic language—a characteristic that endured throughout the century—with women referring to 'irregular cycles', 'returning' or 'bringing on' menstruation. This vernacular may well have been used because many did not consider a pregnancy valid until quickening (when the foetus can be felt moving by the woman in her womb), and/or it was safer and helped maintain secrecy.[46]

[41] Delay, 'Pills, Potions, and Purgatives', pp. 1–22; C. Rattigan, '"Crimes of Passion of the Worst Character": Abortion Cases and Gender in Ireland, 1925–1950', in M. Gialanella Valiulis (ed.), *Gender and Power in Ireland* (Dublin: Irish Academic Press, 2008), pp. 115–40.

[42] Leanne McCormick, '"No Sense of Wrongdoing": Abortion in Belfast 1917–1967', *Journal of Social History*, 49:1 (2015), pp. 124–48, p. 129.

[43] Ibid., p. 130.

[44] McAvoy, 'Before Cadden: Abortion in Mid-Twentieth-Century Ireland', p. 158; Delay, 'Pills, Potions, and Purgatives', p. 8; Benson, 'The Provision of Abortion in Northern Ireland', p. 118; McCormick, 'No Sense of Wrongdoing', pp. 124–48.

[45] Delay, 'Pills, Potions, and Purgatives', p. 13. See also, MacAvoy, 'Before Cadden: Abortion in Mid-Twentieth-Century Ireland'; Benson, 'The Provision of Abortion in Northern Ireland'.

[46] Delay, 'Pills, Potions, and Purgatives,' p. 8; McCormick, 'No Sense of Wrongdoing', p. 128.

Delay argues that the numbers of Irish women who attempted home abortions was high, amounting to 'hundreds, and possibly thousands' prior to the possibility of legal and safe abortions in Britain in 1967. Of the thirty-three cases which she examined in the south of Ireland between 1900 and the 1950s, almost half involved women having ingested something in an attempt to bring on an abortion. The reason provided by women for their preference for pills and remedies was the fear of surgical procedures and the difficulty of the recovery period, which would make secrecy harder to maintain.[47] Furthermore, surgical methods were generally practised by a handful of abortionists who were mostly resident in cities. Accessing services in Dublin or Belfast would have required knowledge, the ability to travel, possibly pay higher fees and have somewhere to stay in order to recover. All of these obstacles made detection more likely and thus, as Delay posits, 'keeping abortion within local networks may have been a strategy…that women adopted to disguise their actions from the police and avoid detection'.[48] It is also highly possible that women regarded pills and herbs as more morally acceptable, allowing them to perceive what they were doing as bringing a period on rather than inducing an abortion.

Of course, women often tried to end a pregnancy by self-violence; the accounts of women falling down stairs, jumping off chairs and subjecting themselves to scalding baths are ubiquitous. Delay noted these methods featured in trials as late as 1961.[49] In many senses these violent interventions symbolise the general disregard for the woman at the heart of the abortion story—some felt self-harm was necessary.[50] Both the violent and ingestion methods of abortion could and did result in women's deaths. While women's attempts at abortion can be interpreted as 'acts of defiance', they clearly demonstrate the desperation and/or fear consequent upon the lack of other safer options.[51]

[47] Delay, 'Pills, Potions, and Purgatives', pp. 1–22.

[48] Ibid., p. 3.

[49] Delay, 'Pills, Potions, and Purgatives', p. 5.

[50] Anne O'Connor notes how old these methods were in Ireland. A. O'Connor, 'Abortion: Myths and Realities from the Irish Folk Tradition', in A. Smyth (ed.), *The Abortion Papers: Ireland* (Dublin: Attic Press, 1992), p. 62.

[51] Delay, 'Pills, Potions, and Purgatives', p. 11.

Table 3.1 Illegal abortions per 100,000 population, 1860–1974

	Eng./Wales	*ROI*	*NI*	*Scot.*
1860–1869	0.0520[a]	0.0337[b]	0.0622[b]	n/a
1890–1899	0.0512	0.0236	0.0161	n/a
1920–1929	0.1679	0.0135	0.0599[c]	0.1192
1950–1959	0.4588	0.0136	0.0939	0.1231
1970–1974	0.1682	–	–	0.0421

[a]Relates to the period 1858–1869; [b]1863–1869; [c]1922–1929. Extracted from Rose, 'Induced Abortion in the Republic of Ireland', p. 246

Back Street Abortions

Rose gauged the level of induced abortion in both the north and south of Ireland using the abortion crime rates known or reported to the police.[52] Figures, measured per 100,000 of the population, revealed a consistently low Irish illegal abortion rate (Table 3.1).

Between 1926 and 1974 there were fifty–eight cases of back street abortions investigated or prosecuted in southern Ireland, but 29% of these occurred in the two-year period from 1942 to 1944 when travel was restricted during the Second World War.[53] One Dublin abortionist and medical examiner confirmed an increase in patients during the war: from 1939 to 1944, he saw at least 30 women, 'married and single, from all parts of Ireland'.[54] This testimony supports McAvoy's contention that by the 1940s there was a network of people in Ireland involved in supplying birth control and information regarding abortion.[55] Similarly, Benson contends that in Northern Ireland: 'The court statements indicate that there was an ongoing system of informal referrals whereby members of the public could access abortions'.[56]

[52]Figures collated from 1858 in England and Wales, from 1867 for England, Wales and Ireland and from 1894 for Scotland. Extracted from Rose, 'Induced Abortion in the Republic of Ireland', p. 245.

[53]Conroy, 'Maternity Confined', p. 131.

[54]McAvoy, 'Before Cadden: Abortion in Mid-Twentieth-Century Ireland', p. 153.

[55]Ibid., p. 160; Conroy, 'Maternity Confined', pp. 127–38, p. 131.

[56]Benson, 'The Provision of Abortion in Northern Ireland', p. 357.

Those prosecuted for performing an abortion were often known to the authorities. Evidence shows it was not only single younger women who sought abortions; half of the women involved in these cases were married with children.[57] For example, an abortion case in the 1940s involved a mother of four children who had been advised not to have any subsequent pregnancies by her doctor. When she became pregnant again she obviously believed that she had no choice but to seek an illegal abortion.[58] She survived the procedure but paid a high fee of £20 for the service (the equivalent of over £1242 in today's values)—for a myriad of reasons, this option was not open to many mothers for whom pregnancy posed a substantial health risk.

The abortion cases that received the most public attention were those which involved a maternal fatality. In 1940, a twenty-five-year-old woman died after undergoing an abortion in County Cork: a maternity nurse and the deceased woman's married boyfriend were subsequently tried. This case received considerable publicity as it involved an extra-marital affair, the tragic death of a young woman and the reputation of a 'respectable' maternity nurse.[59] The most highly publicised, however, was a case involving the abortionist Mary Anne Cadden in 1956, which saw the death of the mother in question and the sentencing of Nurse Cadden to death, although her sentence was commuted to life imprisonment. This case did much to further shape Irish perceptions of abortion as dangerous and illicit.[60] The Cadden case also underscored the vulnerable position of *all* women in Ireland: the pregnant woman who died was not an unmarried mother but a deserted mother of six children. She had been so desperate to avoid a seventh birth that she had travelled to England, not an easy thing to manage with six children at home, but failing to procure an abortion there, she was left with the choice of

[57] McAvoy, 'Before Cadden: Abortion in Mid-Twentieth-Century Ireland', p. 158; Delay, 'Pills, Potions, and Purgatives', p. 11.

[58] McAvoy, 'Before Cadden: Abortion in Mid-Twentieth-Century Ireland', p. 151.

[59] Ibid., p. 161.

[60] Ibid., p. 147. This fear of abortion was cultivated and persisted well into the 1990s in Ireland. For example, in 1993, Carol Walsh, of the British Pregnancy Advisory Service, who had been a counsellor in Liverpool for more than twenty years and had seen hundreds of Irish women in that time, explained: 'a common misconception is that thousands of women die annually on British operating tables and that many are convinced they will never be able to have children'. Rachel Clare, 'Unwanted Pregnancies at Christmas', *Irish Times*, 4 January 1993.

continuing with the pregnancy or risking an illegal abortion in Ireland. She chose the latter and paid with her life. Although Irish culture lauded the large family and venerated the sacrament of marriage, there was little practical support for a deserted mother. Such women did not have the legal right to control their own fertility, to divorce or remarry and were not yet supported by the state.

Although Northern Ireland never policed contraception to the same degree as the Republic of Ireland, abortion at will remained strictly illegal and the implications of the Bourne case were rarely publicly addressed.[61] As noted, the Infant Life (Preservation) Act of 1929, the basis for Bourne's acquittal, was not extended to Northern Ireland.[62] It was not until 1945 that the North updated its abortion legislation with the Criminal Justice Act (Northern Ireland). Section 25 (1) of this legislation dealt with the crime of 'child destruction' with a penalty of 'penal servitude for life'.[63] The act was little used as it only related to late abortions, defined as after 28 weeks by the legislation, and, as with the issue in general, this passed in Stormont without debate.[64]

In spite of its criminalisation, abortion was a reality for some women in Northern Ireland. In 1935, for example, Belfast's Midnight Mission recorded that abortion caused the deaths of nine women in Northern Ireland and reported a further two cases of abortion to the Medical Officer for Health in 1941.[65] Abortion caused five maternal deaths in Northern Ireland in the period from 1964 to 1967 and, as noted, thirty-three cases of illegal abortion were heard in the Belfast courts from 1917 to 1967 but, as in independent Ireland, most illegally procured abortions remained undetected and evaded prosecution.[66] The women who came

[61] See, for example, A. Furedi (ed.), *The Abortion Law in Northern Ireland* (Belfast: Family Planning Association Northern Ireland, 1995); P. Compton, et al., 'Regional Differences in Attitudes to Abortion in Northern Ireland', *Irish Geography*, 19:2 (July 1986), pp. 38–48.

[62] Hug, *The Politics of Sexual Morality in Ireland*, p. 79.

[63] See, www.legislation.gov.uk/apni/1945/15/section/25; L. Smyth, 'The Cultural Politics of Sexuality and Production in Northern Ireland', *Sociology*, 40:4 (2006), p. 666.

[64] Benson, 'The Provision of Abortion in Northern Ireland', p. 232.

[65] See Minutes of Belfast Midnight Mission, 10 September 1941 (PRONI, D2072/1).

[66] McCormick, 'No Sense of Wrongdoing', p. 126. Benson notes that court records are incomplete and his research points to a higher number of cases. He also urges the exploration of lower courts and courts beyond Belfast. Benson, The Provision of Abortion in Northern Ireland, pp. 40–43.

to the attention of the authorities for procuring illegal abortions were mainly working class and from Protestant areas of Belfast. They were also mostly (63.6%) single so the links to the stigma that enveloped illegitimacy remained strong.[67]

Conclusion

Restricted contraceptive provision and the illegality of abortion at will impacted on women's health and cost some women their lives. This was known and acknowledged in both states by medics, judges, clerics and social commentators. Reportage of prosecutions for illegal abortion also allowed this practice to be more widely known, but few came forward to seek a solution that would place women's health centre stage. As Benson notes of Northern Ireland, if formal family planning was too sensitive an issue to publicly engage with until the 1950s, it is little wonder few openly advocated abortions.[68] Consequently, there was no open discussion in Ireland regarding the consequences of such restrictive abortion legalisation on women's health and quality of life. None of the legal cases in either jurisdiction prompted the level of debate engendered by the 1938 Bourne case in Britain, hence there was no space to have a conversation about the impact of pregnancy following rape or the toll of unwanted or repeated pregnancies on women on the island of Ireland.

[67] McCormick, 'No Sense of Wrongdoing', p. 139.

[68] See Benson, 'The Provision of Abortion in Northern Ireland'.

CHAPTER 4

Contraceptive Mentalities, 1960s–1980s

Abstract Artificial birth control was largely condemned and unavailable in Northern Ireland until the late 1960s and prohibited in the Republic of Ireland until 1979. In both states the issue continued to be conflated with abortion and considered largely within the realm of morality rather than health care until the 1970s. This chapter examines the debates on the liberalisation of birth control in the 1960s and 1970s with a view to understanding the history of reproductive rights on the island. It explores how this reframing of the birth control issue contributed to a determination by well-organised conservative groups to ensure that Ireland did not witness a similar reform of abortion laws on the island.

Keywords Contraception · Birth control · Reproductive rights · Second Vatican Council · Humanae Vitae · Coitus interruptus

Artificial birth control was largely condemned and unavailable in Northern Ireland until the late 1960s and prohibited in the Republic of Ireland until 1979. In both states, the issue continued to be conflated with abortion and considered largely within the realm of morality rather than health care until the 1970s. In the Republic of Ireland, those opposed to the legalisation of birth control framed it as a gateway to abortion and promiscuity, which would erode the very foundations of the state. In Northern Ireland similar concerns emerged against

L. Earner-Byrne and D. Urquhart, *The Irish Abortion Journey, 1920–2018*, Genders and Sexualities in History,
https://doi.org/10.1007/978-3-030-03855-7_4

a backdrop of a supposed moral consensus which bridged the religious divide: northern Protestants and Catholics appeared largely united in their fear of sexual promiscuity and abhorrence of abortion. This chapter examines birth control debates in the 1960s and 1970s with a view to understanding the history of reproductive rights on the island and how they facilitated the creation of some of the most restrictive abortion regimes in Europe in two ostensibly very different states. After the legalisation of abortion in Britain in 1967, the shadow of abortion in Ireland, in the form of thousands of clandestine journeys to Britain, contributed to a gradual social reconsideration of the impact of moral intolerance, in particular, on single mothers and their children. While this realisation resulted in more support for the unmarried mother and a greater acceptance of adoption, it did not lead to a fundamental change of opinion regarding women's rights to bodily autonomy. In fact, this reframing of the birth control issue contributed to a determination by well-organised conservative groups to ensure that Ireland did not witness a similar reform of abortion laws.

Shifting Ground: Ireland Since the 1960s

The island of Ireland was not immune to the reforming energies of the 1960s.[1] During this period the island completed its transition from a predominantly rural to an urban society. While emigration persisted as a real and present social reality, more young people remained in the country than ever before and those that stayed were better educated. Furthermore, the opening of educational opportunities embraced more girls than boys. By the 1960s 1 in 5 boys and girls completed secondary school, with girls in the slight minority; by 1980 this was inverted with two-thirds of girls compared to a half of boys sitting their final secondary school exams. In 1971 women made up almost 38% of third-level students in the Republic; by 1981 this had increased to 44%.[2] Young

[1] See M. E. Daly, *Sixties Ireland: Reshaping the Economy, State and Society, 1957–1973* (Cambridge: Cambridge University Press, 2016); C. Holohan, *Reframing Irish Youth in the Sixties* (Liverpool: Liverpool University Press, 2018).

[2] H. Burke, 'Continuity and Change: The Life Cycle of Irish Women in the 1980s', *The Changing Family* (Family Studies Unit, UCD, 1984), pp. 39–57, p. 44. This Family Studies Unit in UCD contributed a tremendous amount to our understanding of a changing society in the Republic of Ireland. It had no equivalent in Northern Ireland.

people in Northern Ireland benefited from developments following the Northern Ireland Education Act of 1947 and an increase in the school leaving age to 16 in 1972, both of which resulted in gradual increases in the numbers completing secondary school. The educational gender-gap also narrowed considerably during the 1960s and 1970s, but Northern Ireland remained slightly behind the Republic in this regard following instead similar patterns to industrialised England.[3]

There were also changes in sexual decision-making with Irish people on both sides of the border marrying younger and having fewer children.[4] In the Republic, the percentage of families with ten or more children dropped from 14% in 1911 to 3% in 1971.[5] In both Northern Ireland and the Republic of Ireland, fertility declined faster among Protestants than among Catholics, although the gap between the denominations lessened by the 1980s.[6] Another factor that had a bearing on intimate decisions was the reduction in the age gap between married couples, particularly in the Republic. The percentage of marriages where the bride and groom were the same age doubled between 1946 and 1979 rising to 13%, with the age gap in all marriages narrowing considerably.[7] Writing in 1984, the sociologist Patrick Clancy described these changes in Irish family life as a 'demographic transformation', which reflected a 'significant shift in the culture and value system of our society'.[8]

Indeed, a study of twenty-nine Catholic families who were first-generation Dubliners between 1949 and 1950 recorded the stirrings of these changes. The study found the 'New Dubliner father' was 'more open and frank than the countryman in discussing sex and the problems of sexual instruction and morality, and he tends to take a more reasoned, rather than a sheer authoritarian, approach to the religious instruction

[3] R. Breen, A. F. Heath, and C. Whelan, 'Inequality in Ireland, North and South', in R. Breen, A. Health, and C. Whelan (eds), *Ireland, North and South, Perspectives from Social Sciences* (Oxford: Oxford University Press, 1999), pp. 187–213, p. 195, p. 206.

[4] Urquhart, 'Gender, Family and Sexuality in Ulster, 1800–2000', pp. 246–59.

[5] P. Clancy, 'Demographic Changes and the Irish Family', *The Changing Family* (Family Studies Unit, UCD, 1984), pp. 1–38, p. 21.

[6] Urquhart, 'Gender, Family and Sexuality', p. 247.

[7] Clancy, 'Demographic Changes and the Irish Family', p. 12.

[8] Ibid., p. 31.

of his children'.[9] However, values died hard, with parents in the study lamenting their own sexual ignorance upon marriage, but not yet comfortable to instruct their children.[10] These new Dubliners were the transitional generation moving from the country to the city, from authoritarianism to negotiation, from silence to debate. While there was embarrassment and shame about sex, there was also anger about a culture that had kept people sexually ignorant. As one wife explained: 'I think that it was really sinful that I was allowed to marry as ignorant and as innocent as I was about the whole matter'. Another woman described the losing of her virginity upon marriage as the 'greatest loss of her life' and others admitted sex was 'repulsive'. Men were not immune to such conflicted feelings, with one stating: 'We Irish have very peculiar ideas on the subject of sex, despite what anybody might say. Back of everybody's mind is the notion that there is something wrong with it, something bad'. Another husband admitted his wife had to teach him about the marriage act.[11]

The Second Vatican Council (1962–1965) generated much anticipation about the possibility of change in Catholic Church teachings regarding marriage and the use of artificial birth control. The Republic's Minister for Justice, Brian Lenihan summed up the sense of expectation when he observed: 'the whole subject of contraception is very much a live issue at the moment and…Catholics were awaiting a definitive ruling on the subject'.[12] However, his words also underscored the state's reluctance to move on the issue until papal approval was forthcoming. The Pope's ruling came in the form of the encyclical *Humanae Vitae* [On Human Life] in 1968, which reaffirmed the Catholic Church's unequivocal ban on the triumvirate of 'abortion, contraception and divorce, linking the three issues in a moral framework that should be defended'.[13] The impact of unrealised expectations was tangible. Dorine Rohan, who travelled around Ireland in the late 1960s exploring Irish marriage, explained: 'The reactions in Ireland to the Encyclical have been varied…

[9] A. J. Humphreys, *New Dubliners: Urbanization and the Irish Family* (London: Routledge and Kegan Paul PLC, 1966), p. 38.

[10] Ibid., p. 120.

[11] Ibid., p. 139.

[12] 'Majority are in favour of censorship', *Irish Press*, 11 May 1967.

[13] B. Girvin, 'Contraception, Moral Panic and Social Change in Ireland, 1969–79', *Irish Political Studies*, 23: 4 (2008), pp. 555–76, p. 565.

Anger, sadness, astonishment, relief have been felt and expressed by every sphere of the community…many who have been practising birth control will not return to the fold'.[14] Mary O'Rourke, then a teacher, but better known as a politician and minister in several governments, noted: 'I clearly remember the sense of hope not being realised'.[15] And, as Patsy McGarry astutely observed, 'it could have been so different'[16]: the possibilities of science, most pertinently in the form of the contraceptive pill and the change in women's position in society, all contributed to sense of 'a moment' when lives could have been transformed. O'Rourke recalled that around that time a young married woman with six children sought refuge in her house after being beaten by her husband. When she was leaving the next day, O'Rourke gave her a copy of *Hibernia* magazine with an advertisement for condoms which would be sent to readers for a £1. The grateful woman circulated this among her female network, which prompted a visit to O'Rourke by the local priest. When the priest chastised O'Rourke for distributing birth control information, she asked: 'Well, what would you do?' To which the priest merely parroted the church teaching: 'Marriage is for procreation'.[17] O'Rourke's vignette is highly revealing as it underscores that local female networks were acting as surrogate sources of consolation, advice and support in a society whose values were moving beyond the teachings of the main church.

There is also evidence to suggest that some priests were not immune to the suffering that the ban on contraception caused to their female parishioners. Rohan, for example, claimed that in the privacy of the confession box, some priests advised mothers to take the pill.[18] She testified that many Irish people believed four children comprised the ideal family size and that spacing and/or limiting one's family was legitimate. As one angry mother told her: 'It is all very well saying the Lord will provide, all He provided me with was ten children. I'll see my daughters don't go through the same. I'd rather them enter a convent'.[19] Rohan confirmed that coitus interruptus (although a mortal sin according to

[14] D. Rohan, *Marriage Irish Style* (Cork: Mercier Press, 1969), p. 92.

[15] P. McGarry, 'How Humanae Vitae Crushed the Hopes of Millions of Catholics', *Irish Times*, 28 July 2018.

[16] Ibid.

[17] McGarry, 'How Humanae Vitae Crushed the Hopes of Millions of Catholics'.

[18] Rohan, *Marriage Irish Style*, p. 93.

[19] Ibid., p. 101.

Catholic teaching) was the most common method of birth control as the rhythm method was complicated and often unsuccessful.[20] One woman confided: 'We have had four children in five years, and we don't want any more for the moment – but my husband is very decent, he uses the withdrawal method'.[21] However, for others such marital co-operation could not be elicited even under clerical pressure. As a forty-two-year-old mother of nine explained: 'himself wouldn't cooperate – he wouldn't listen to a priest or anything. I hear people talk about the spare room, but sure where would I get a spare room, in the name of God?'[22]

The Irish Catholic hierarchy appeared immune to such arguments, issuing several statements and pastorals between 1971 and 1978 reiterating prohibitive teachings. One contemporary observer astutely argued that this was an indication of the difficulty the church faced in clarifying its role in a changing society.[23] One such pastoral issued in March 1971 attempted to prevent the state from responding to the expectations for contraceptive reform which grew in the 1960s: 'It may well come to pass that, in the present climate of emotional thinking and pressure, legislation could be enacted that will offend the objective moral law…Such a measure would be an insult to our Faith; it would without question be gravely damaging to morality, private and public'.[24] There were lay groups which supported the church hierarchy's inflexible position, such as a group describing itself as 'a team of Catholic parents', which railed against what it depicted as a 'barrage of brain-washing from the media in favour of contraception and its legalization in Ireland' since *Humanae Vitae*.[25] This group articulated what was to become an enduring argument among Catholic theologians, clerics and conservative lay groups against birth control, when it claimed: 'In practice, far from preventing the conception of unwanted children, contraception and the development of the contraceptive mentality combine to make illegitimacy such a problem that legalized abortion is then demanded as the only means of

[20] Ibid., p. 78.
[21] Ibid., p. 67.
[22] Ibid., pp. 37–38.
[23] L. Ryan, 'Church and Politics', *Furrow*, 30:1 (January 1979), pp. 3–18.
[24] Cited in A Team of Catholic Parents, *Is Contraception the Answer?* (February 1974), p. 2.
[25] Ibid.

solving it'.[26] This group rejected social arguments, decrying 'the horde of hypothetical women with sixteen children, living in one room with a drunken, unemployed husband'.[27] However, these Catholic parents were, in fact, highlighting the increasingly prevalent tendency in public debate to link poverty and relentless pregnancies with a new narrative of civil rights. The group's case against 'the media' was to become a central plank of conservative arguments against women's reproductive freedom, which survives to the present day.

A Right to Family Privacy

It was clear that some Irish people, like O'Rourke's neighbour, were exercising their own agency and controlling their fertility through the post. The Northern Irish Family Planning Association (NIFPA), established in 1965, also dealt with a 'constant stream of letters from people living in Southern Ireland asking for advice' on birth control. NIFPA subsequently sent supplies over the border by post addressed by hand to avert the suspicion of customs.[28] Any suggestion of a wholesale societal conversion to artificial birth control would be misleading, but there is strong evidence of people wishing to, and actually, limiting family size through various means. While the majority of people still considered birth control to be a moral rather than a medical or rights issue, many were also coming to regard the question as one of private conscience and there was a greater understanding for the 'hard cases'. This was aided by informed conscience within the Catholic Church, as well as an increase in the numbers of educated young people who were staying in or returning to Ireland throughout the 1960s and 1970s. Many of Ireland's youth began to espouse different priorities and values relating to gender, sexuality and the place of religion in public life and social policy.[29] For example, the emergence of the second-wave women's movement in the early 1970s provided a focus for differing understandings of gender and

[26] Ibid, p. 5. This argument was repeated in 2018 by Catholic Bishop of Elphin Kevin Doran, who used the phrase 'contraceptive mentality' which he linked to support for same-sex marriage. C. Gleeson, 'Principles of Contraceptive Ban 'Ignored for Too Long', Says Bishop', *Irish Times*, 4 August 2018.

[27] A Team of Catholic Parents, *Is Contraception the Answer?* p. 2.

[28] McCormick, 'The Scarlet Woman in Person', p. 356.

[29] See, Holohan, *Reframing Irish Youth in the Sixties*.

morality.[30] It is no coincidence that the new movement promoted the rights of single mothers and made the legalisation of birth control a core aim by highlighting the hypocrisy of a country that could only maintain its moral absolutism because Irish people accessed solutions outside the state.[31] In May 1971, the Irish Women's Liberation Movement [hereafter IWLM] organised a trip to Belfast to buy birth control, in order to return to Dublin, declare their illegal import and insist that the Irish custom officers enforce the law. This became known as the 'contraceptive train' and represented the new movement's 'direct action tactics'.[32] This raised awareness in the south, but it also reinforced the somewhat exaggerated notion of the North's liberalism.

In the same year, the McGee case coalesced the various factors pushing for the legalisation of birth control in the Republic. A twenty-seven-year-old mother of four, Mrs. McGee, was advised by her doctor to avoid another pregnancy after experiencing a stroke during a previous pregnancy.[33] She attempted to import contraceptives via the post, but her order was confiscated under the 1935 Criminal Law Amendment Act, which made the importation of birth control material illegal. In 1971, represented by the feminist and Senator Mary Robinson, she took a case against the Attorney General and the revenue, challenging the legality of the seizure.[34] While the High Court rejected her case in 1973, the Supreme Court, embracing the US ruling of *Griswold v Connecticut*,[35] found in her favour in the following year on the basis that married couples had the right to make private decisions regarding their family planning.[36]

[30] Hug, *The Politics of Sexual Morality in Ireland*, pp. 109–40. One of the best accounts of this second-wave movement is L. Connolly, *The Irish Women's Movement: From Revolution to Devolution* (Basingstoke and New York: Palgrave, 2002).

[31] Connolly, *The Irish Women's Movement*, p. 120.

[32] For analysis of the significance of this event and the wider movement see, Connolly, *The Irish Women's Movement*, pp. 111–29.

[33] See, Mary McGee Plaintiff v. THE ATTORNEY GENERAL and THE REVENUE COMMISSIONERS Defendants [1971 No. 2314 P].

[34] Ibid.

[35] In 1965 in the *Griswold v Connecticut* case, the American Supreme Court ruled that a state's ban on the use of contraceptives violated a couple's right to marital privacy.

[36] M. Fox and T. Murphy, 'Irish Abortion: Seeking Refuge in a Jurisprudence of Doubt and Delegation', *Journal of Law and Society*, 19:4 (1992), pp. 454–66, p. 455.

This ruling was pivotal in forcing the Irish government into action on the issue of birth control.[37]

Many in Irish society were nervous about the implications of the McGee ruling, fearful it might lead to the legalisation of contraception for all sections of society and, in consequence, encourage promiscuity. An editorial in the *Irish Medical Association* journal reflected this general anxiety: 'While doctors in Ireland appear to support, at least in principle, the right of married couples to regulate family size by the use of contraceptives…in other countries…contraception has been followed by a sharp decline in standards of sexual morality, [and] a rise in the incidence of venereal disease to epidemic proportions'.[38] The conservative Catholic forces that wished to maintain the *status quo* also quickly identified the legalisation of birth control as a gateway to abortion. When, in 1971, the Republic's Minister for Health, Erskine Childers, was asked if, in view of the numbers of Irish women travelling to Britain for abortions, he would consider 'a national family planning education programme', he responded: 'The facts show that in countries where national family planning has been advanced to a tremendous extent, the abortion rate has risen'.[39]

Over the preceding years, as various bills were brought before the Irish parliament in an attempt to find legislation that would finally satisfy the conservative polity, the introduction of contraception was presented as a threat to the state, to the quality of life in Ireland, to reconciliation with Northern Ireland and to the entire national project that had resulted in the creation of the Republic. The idea of a politically independent and morally superior Ireland was often to the fore. Britain, by comparison, was cast as sexually wanton and materialistic. The idea that Ireland was somehow uniquely sexually abstemious and moral was widely shared. However, during the 1960s and 1970s, the two main political parties began to diverge on the extent to which they believed state policy should reinforce religious morality. In this realignment, the centre-right party, Fianna Fáil sought to portray itself as the guardian of these foundational

[37] B. Girvin, 'An Irish Solution to an Irish Problem: Catholicism, Contraception and Change, 1922–1979', *Contemporary European History*, 27:1 (2018), pp. 1–22, p. 15.

[38] Editorial, *Journal of the Irish Medical Association*, 66 (March 1973), p. 140.

[39] Questions. Oral Answers. Family Planning Education. *Dáil Éireann Debate*, col. 1320, vol. 261, no. 8, 13 June 1973.

values, in its bid to shore up rural and conservative support.[40] In the late 1960s, Fine Gael began to adopt a more liberal economic and social outlook including an emphasis on private conscience and a re-examination of the role of the state in issues relating to sexual morality.[41] The party's changing attitudes to sexual morality, including the issue of divorce, were also influenced by a somewhat misplaced belief that reconciliation with Northern Ireland would be advanced if the Republic's laws appeared less 'Catholic' in relation to these issues. This particular point of view gained little traction in Fianna Fáil, which tended to articulate an unabashed pride in the Republic's moral conservatism. During one particularly heated parliamentary debate in 1974, Fianna Fáil's Michael Kitt, for example, claimed that Fine Gael was trying to bring 'in a contraception Bill that will ruin the quality of life…for which generations fought and died'.[42] While internal forces influenced these political arguments regarding sexual freedom, international developments also impacted. For example, the significance of the *Roe v Wade* Supreme Court ruling in the US, where the plaintiff's right to privacy extended to her right to an abortion, was not lost in Ireland. Fianna Fáil's Oliver J. Flanagan emphasised the importance of these developments:

> It is no harm to mention that the American Supreme Court have also unwrapped the box of privacy in regard to the rights of citizens…They

[40]Fianna Fáil was established when the Sinn Féin party split in 1926. The former quickly became one of the most important political parties in the state winning the first overall majority in parliament in 1933. The party remained in government for sixteen years between 1932 and 1948 and again between 1957 and 1973. See, J. Coakley, Fianna Fáil, S. J. Connolly (ed.), *The Oxford Companion to Irish History* (Oxford: Oxford University Press, 1998), pp. 191–92. See also, R. Dunphy, *The Making of Fianna Fáil: Power in Ireland, 1923–1948* (Oxford: Oxford University Press, 1995).

[41]Fine Gael was founded in 1923 as Cumann na nGaedheal and led the Irish Free State through its first ten years of existence. However, after this point the party struggled to gain power unless in a coalition government with other smaller parties. See, J. Coakley, 'Fine Gael', in Connolly (ed.), *The Oxford Companion to Irish History*, pp. 194–95. See also, C. Meehan, *A Just Society for Ireland?1964–1987* (London: Palgrave Macmillan, 2013).

[42]Control of Importation, Sale and Manufacture of Contraceptives Bill, 1974: Second Stage (resumed). *Dáil Éireann Debate*, col. 919, vol. 274, no. 6, 11 July 1974. On Fianna Fáil's position, see Hug, *The Politics of Sexual Morality*, pp. 105–7.

> found in it was the right of contraception for the unmarried, the right of pornography and also the right of abortion.[43]

Irrespective of strong political opposition, particularly within Fianna Fáil, the Catholic hierarchy and vocal sections of the laity, there was an acknowledgement that some legal change would have to occur to reflect the McGee ruling. By 1976 the radical Irishwomen United [hereafter IWU] had made free legal contraception a main goal with the formation of the Contraceptive Action Campaign [hereafter CAP].[44] This group along with other organisation such as the Well Woman Centre and the Family Planning Clinics began providing contraceptives to their clients. CAP was particularly pro-active in organising street demonstrations and rising public awareness (Fig. 4.1). The legislation that was finally introduced in 1979 responded to both the concerns about a 'permissive' society *and* the demands for change, by effectively restricting access to contraceptives to married couples via prescription. This was hardly revolutionary, but social change rarely comes as a rupture. It was, thus, fittingly a Fianna Fáil government that devised the compromise and the minister responsible, Charles J. Haughey was at pains to note 'the House did not deal with abortion, but contraception'. As the *Irish Times* reported, he was 'concerned not to impinge on the 1861 Criminal Law Amendment Act which forbade abortion and which had stood the test of time'.[45]

The 1979 legislation made doctors responsible for deciding if a couple had a *bona fide* family planning or medical reasons for using birth control.[46] There is little doubt that doctors were placed in this position not because the issue was being reframed as a health issue, but because of their social status; they were safe 'moral arbiters'.[47] Ultimately, as

[43] Control of Importation, Sale and Manufacture of Contraceptives Bill, 1974, col. 943, vol. 274, no. 6 (11 July 1974).

[44] Connolly, *The Irish Women's Movement*, p. 90. Interestingly, many women involved in IWU and CAP went on to prominence in the Women's Right to Choose organisation and other pro-choice groups.

[45] 'Contraception Bill Reaches Final Stages', *Irish Times*, 13 July 1979.

[46] See, Health (Family Planning) Act, 1979, Section 4 (4), http://www.irishstatutebook.ie/eli/1979/act/20/enacted/en/html.

[47] It is important to note that many doctors were not happy about being put in this position.

Fig. 4.1 Contraception Action Campaign (CAP) demonstration, Dublin, 2 December 1978. Photo by Derek Speirs

Senator Gemma Hussey pointed out, the act created another layer of, usually male, power to mediate women's decisions about their bodies: 'No woman should have to live in fear of pregnancy because of either an unreliable husband or an unco-operative doctor'.[48] Undoubtedly, many wives were in this position, as one forty-nine-year-old woman of a 'large grown-up family' wrote to the magazine *Woman's Way* in 1983: 'I'm off the pill, but worry about becoming pregnant as my husband will not use a condom'.[49] At a one-day conference in opposition to the new family planning legislation, Senator Catherine McGuinness queried what right the 'Government had to interfere in private morality'?[50] At the same gathering, it was pointed out that denying access to birth control would, ironically 'either mean that there would be more children born to parents already stretched to capacity to cope with their existing children', or, in

[48]G. Hussey, Health and Family Planning Bill, 1978: Second Stage (resumed). *Seanad Éireann Debate*, col. 736, vol. 92, no. 9 (4 July 1979).

[49]'Risk of Pregnancy': Patients' Postbox, *Woman's Way*, 8 July 1983, p. 51.

[50]M. Foley, 'Group Defies Family Planning', *Irish Times*, 3 November 1980.

reference to the fact that Irish women travelled to Britain to have abortions, more would '"take the Liverpool boat" – Ireland's escape route'.[51]

In the 1980s there was evidence that birth control continued to be difficult to access for many, particularly rural, Irish women: in 1983, feminist Nell McCafferty noted that not one pharmacy in a small Kerry town stocked contraception.[52] However, Máire Nic Ghiolla Phádraig, writing in 1984, agreed that 'a sizeable number of doctors and chemists have refused to exercise their rights under the Act, [but] it is probably true to say that the supply of contraceptives is more extensive than ever before ... Natural family planning instruction has also become more diversified and more widely available'.[53] Commenting on doctors' role in assessing *bona fide* access to contraceptives, she suggested this was 'probably more honoured in the breach than in the observance', pointing out there was only one prosecution under the legislation by the mid-1980s.[54] Despite initial disappointment among feminists and liberals in Ireland, in the long run it was significant that the issue of birth control was now the remit of the Department of Health rather than Justice as this break was irreversible and represented an acceptance that family planning services were a part of health care. As Nic Ghiolla Phádraig speculated, 'the medicalisation of contraception may help others to overcome their reticence'.[55] However, the Department of Health only slowly embraced its new responsibility for birth control[56]: a 1987 study of maternity and infant care schemes noted that 48% of women had received no family planning advice.[57] Clearly, as it was not obligatory to supply this service to Irish women, the Department of Health was in no hurry to do so. It

[51] Labour Councillor Mary Freehill cited in Michael Foley, 'Group Defies Family Planning', *Irish Times*, 3 November 1980.

[52] N. McCafferty, *A Woman to Blame: The Kerry Babies Case* (Dublin: Attic Press, 1985), p. 31.

[53] M. Nic Ghiolla Phádraig, 'Social and Cultural Factors in Family Planning', *The Changing Family* (Dublin: Family Studies Unit, UCD, 1984), pp. 58–97, p. 68.

[54] Ibid., p. 81.

[55] Ibid., p. 93.

[56] Under Section 2 of the 1979 Act, the minister was responsible for providing 'orderly organization of family planning services', and the provision of 'comprehensive natural family planning services'.

[57] Earner-Byrne, 'Twixt God and Geography: The Development of Maternity Services in Twentieth-Century Ireland', p. 112.

was not until 1993 that Irish health boards were legally obliged to provide family planning services.[58]

A Liberal North?

While Northern Ireland was often represented as a safe house across the border for liberal minds, this was another distortion. Birth control had never been illegal in Northern Ireland, but it was also not embraced in any meaningful way by either citizens or state prior to the 1970s, when family size began its consistent decline.[59] However, the work of Dr. Olive Anderson, medical officer to a new family planning clinic at the Royal Maternity Hospital in Belfast in 1940, was pioneering in widening both access to and a gradual acceptance of contraception. This clinic gave informal family planning advice to medically-referred maternity patients. In 1950 Anderson noted that she 'smuggled in one or two patients [in] from local GPs', revealing that a clandestine approach to contraception was still required. Anderson also co-founded (with Dr. Charlotte Arnold, formerly of the Mothers' Clinic) the Belfast Women's Welfare Clinic in the south of the city in 1951, which moved to Belfast City Hospital in 1959. Significantly, the clinic did not use marriage as a qualifier for contraceptive advice. By 1960 56.1% of patients coming to this clinic were from Belfast with the remainder drawn from across Northern Ireland. Some travelled 70 miles to access the clinic's services providing yet another indication of the increasing demand to plan and space births. However, such journeys were indicative of the many black spots in the provision of birth control in Northern Ireland throughout the 1960s. Anderson acknowledged that religion remained 'the stumbling block',[60] referring, in particular, to opposition from the Catholic Church and the more Calvinist elements of Protestantism. Thus, just as Moya Woodside had observed in the 1930s and 1940s, religious sensitivities in Northern Ireland made cross-community action in relation to women's health difficult. In 1962, the *Belfast Telegraph* described the attitude in Northern Ireland to birth control as 'befogged and confused

[58] See, Health (Family Planning) (Amendment) Act, 1992, http://www.irishstatutebook.ie/eli/1992/act/20/section/8/enacted/en/html#sec8.

[59] Urquhart, 'Gender, Family and Sexuality', pp. 246–59, p. 254.

[60] Cited in McCormick, 'The Scarlet Woman', pp. 346, 348. For figures, see ibid., p. 353.

with prejudice and muddled thinking'.[61] While in 1966, a BBC Inquiry Programme told its audience: 'In Northern Ireland, family planning has a nasty taste – people don't like to talk about it…even the medical profession, in certain instances are reluctant to recommend that their patient should visit a clinic for family planning service'.[62]

Despite this, by the late 1960s there were seven clinics in Northern Ireland and four new clinics planned. NIFPA was buoyant, believing that that attitudes towards birth control were 'changing…rapidly', but 'they were still very concerned about making the addresses of [the] clinics widely known'.[63] Indeed, NIFPA chair, Dr. Joyce Neill, addressing the body's first public meeting in Belfast in 1965, echoed Anderson in highlighting the specific religious challenges: 'Northern Ireland family planning clinics must be prepared to advise Roman Catholic patients on methods of family planning acceptable to their beliefs'.[64] The rhythm method as well as artificial contraceptives was therefore prescribed.[65] From 1963 to 1964, 2996 patients 'from all denominations' with a 'proportion of Catholics who come to be instructed in their Church's approved rhythm method; and also some [who] ask about mechanical forms of contraception' attended NIFPA clinics.[66] Following the ruling of the Family Planning Association in London, women who were soon to marry were also seen in Northern Ireland, with two visits prior to marriage advised. Moreover, in a press interview in 1965, one of the NIFPA directors conceded that there might be additional 'individual circumstances where advice could be given', indicating a willingness to respect individual people's needs.[67]

[61] Ibid., p. 352.

[62] Script of BBC 'Inquiry Programme', 14 January 1966. Cited in McCormick, *Regulating Sexuality*, p. 186.

[63] Minutes of NIFPA, 1 March and 6 December 1966, PRONI, D3543/2/2.

[64] *Belfast Telegraph*, 12 November 1965.

[65] MP Harry Diamond cited in McCormick, 'The Scarlet Woman', p. 351.

[66] *Belfast Telegraph*, 22 March 1965. Board members of the NIFPA were, however, disappointed by the level of publicity and BBC coverage generated by their first meeting with the latter refusing to advertise 'a controversial cause'. See Minutes of NIFPA, 22 November 1965, PRONI, D3543/2/2. Patients paid for contraceptive devices with 15/1 estimated as the cost of a first visit. But, fees would be waived if referred for medical reasons or for 'those patients whose husbands are unemployed or who have large families and cannot afford to pay', Minutes of NIFPA, 1965, PRONI, D3543/2/1.

[67] *Belfast Telegraph*, 22 March 1965.

When the Northern Irish Minister of Health finally provided the NIFPA with a grant in 1968, the one voice raised in opposition was from a Republican Labour party representative, who echoed sentiments heard ad nauseam in the Republic of Ireland, that birth control was a gateway to abortion and promoted sexual promiscuity that would lead to an increase in sexually transmitted diseases.[68] The pill was introduced into clinical practice in Northern Ireland in 1963, and in 1969, the provisions of the 1967 National Health Service (Family Planning) Act were applied to Northern Ireland. This permitted local authorities to provide contraception on social and medical grounds irrespective of the marital status of clients.[69] With the onus now on local health authorities to provide family planning services, as NIFPA recorded, there were 'great battles in some cases' and the need for 'dialogue between different points of view especially acceptance of the R. C. [Roman Catholic] standpoint' continued.[70] Some of the stigma attached to family planning was, however, evidently in decline: NIFPA saw an annual increase of 800 new patients and 3000 attendances in 1967.[71] Nonetheless, the average family size in Northern Ireland remained considerably higher than for the rest of the UK: in 1971 it was recorded at 3.4 compared to 2.9 for Britain. The pace of family planning development increased in Northern Ireland through the 1970s indicating growing acceptance. By 1973 NIFPA had thirty-eight family planning clinics and free NHS-funded family planning services were available in Northern Ireland by 1974, although the lack of public discourse on the issue hints at a lingering disquiet.[72] Nonetheless, in a continuation of Anderson and Arnold's work, family planning became increasingly integrated into the NHS with hospitals and GPs' clinics as the key sites of provision; by 1974 local authorities had taken over all former NIFPA clinics and they began providing free

[68] McCormick, 'The Scarlet Woman', p. 354.

[69] Ibid., pp. 346, 353.

[70] Minutes of NIFPA, 1965, PRONI, D3543/2/1. For example, McCormick charts the difficulties faced in establishing family planning clinics in Derry. McCormick, 'The Scarlet Woman', pp. 354–55.

[71] 40 new members of NIFPA were also recorded. NIFPA annual report, 1967, PRONI, D3543/2/2.

[72] J. F. O'Sullivan, 'The History of Obstetrics in Northern Ireland, 1921–1992', *UMJ*, 70:2 (November 2001), pp. 95–101, p. 99.

contraceptives in the following year.[73] Reports which stressed the deleterious impact of relentless pregnancies on women's health also helped in rendering birth control more acceptable. In 1978 the Northern Ireland Department of Health and Social Services concluded that 'a mother able to space her children is likely to be healthier during pregnancy' and thus less likely to develop conditions like anaemia and deliver a low birth weight baby.[74]

However, there were signs that Northern Irish women still faced many obstacles to gaining control of their fertility including values that prioritised chastity and procreation within marriage. Writing in 1977, Lynda Edgerton noted: 'It is my opinion that many Northern Ireland working-class women do not view sex as an enjoyable act. A number of women who I spoke to in both Protestant and Catholic areas of Belfast all gave this impression'.[75] Similar values about sex outside marriage were widely shared in Northern Ireland and many young people still married relatively ignorant of the workings of their own bodies. As Edgerton observed, 'several of the young women I spoke to had not experienced sex before marriage and were embarrassed and ashamed to talk about it'.[76] She also offered a thought-provoking perspective on gender-relations in a society mired in conflict: 'Another effect of internment was that it gave the women a break from pregnancy.'[77] This would indicate that some Northern Irish women remained relatively powerless to control their fertility within marriage.

Conclusion

What emerged in both jurisdictions was an acknowledgement that contraception was acceptable within marriage and that this should be dictated by the needs of the individual rather than state policy. While both states shared a resistance to the idea that birth control was acceptable for unmarried people, Northern Ireland conceded this moral point

[73] NIFPA ceased operations in 1977.

[74] Community Health, Infant Mortality, Northern Ireland Department of Health and Social Services, 1978–1979, PRONI, HSS/13/35/46.

[75] L. Edgerton, 'Examination of the Role of Northern Irish Women in Their Domestic, Social and Political Life, 1967–1977' (unpublished BA thesis, QUB, 1977), p. 11

[76] Ibid.

[77] Ibid., p. 26.

before the Republic of Ireland. However, the recasting of contraception as a civil right was significant in both states. There is, nonetheless, little doubt that this, and the gradual reframing of morality as a private rather than a public issue, contributed to a campaign by organised and effective conservative groups to ensure that abortion would not be legalised on the island of Ireland. This was contingent on a stubborn refusal to even engage with the ongoing reality of abortions in both states and beyond their borders, an ambivalence that the 1967 Abortion Act in Britain would throw into sharp relief.

CHAPTER 5

Pro-life States of Mind, 1967–2000s

Abstract The introduction of the Abortion Act of 1967 in Britain had significant impact on the lives of women on the island of Ireland who could, and did, travel for legal and safe abortions. However, it also facilitated Ireland's continued evasion of complex issues related to pregnancy, thus forcing women to seek solutions to their unwanted, unsafe or unviable pregnancies beyond the moral gaze of both states. While there were significant differences in each state's handling of these issues, in both cases the policy decisions made in relation to abortion were not woman-centred and were often driven by highly organised conservative forces adept at using politics for ideological purposes. This chapter analyses the moral dynamics of both states exploring the nuances that differentiated them and the cultural forces that made them so similar. It argues that geography and politics were essential to the sustained and successful opposition to abortion in both jurisdictions: they could both export the abortion issue and use women's bodies for political ends.

Keywords Abortion Act of 1967 · 'Good faith' · Conservative · Pro-life · Pro-choice · Constitutional amendment · 'X' case

The British Abortion Act of 1967 was not extended to Northern Ireland and had no legal impact on the situation in the Republic of Ireland. However, it revolutionised the options open to women on the island of

L. Earner-Byrne and D. Urquhart, *The Irish Abortion Journey, 1920–2018*, Genders and Sexualities in History, https://doi.org/10.1007/978-3-030-03855-7_5

Ireland who could, and did, travel to avail of legal and safe abortions. The legalisation of abortion in Britain also facilitated Ireland's continued evasion of complex issues related to pregnancy, thus forcing women to seek solutions to their unwanted, unsafe or unviable pregnancies beyond the moral gaze of both states. While there were significant differences in each state's handling of these issues, in both cases the policy decisions made in relation to abortion were not woman-centred and were often driven by highly organised conservative forces adept at using politics for ideological purposes. This chapter analyses the moral dynamics of both states, exploring the nuances that differentiated them and the cultural forces that made them so similar. It argues that geography and politics were essential to the sustained and successful opposition to abortion in both jurisdictions: each state could export the abortion issue and use their control of women's bodies for political ends.

'Good Faith' Abortion in Northern Ireland

In January 1969, the Attorney General for Northern Ireland explained that the Abortion Act of 1967 should not be extended to the province because 'the feelings of many people here on these matters do not coincide fully with those of the people in Great Britain'. Harold Ian McClure, the Ulster Unionist MP for Queen's University and a Fellow of the Royal College of Obstetricians and Gynaecologists, affirmed the Attorney General's declaration, adding 'no further legislation is required on this side of the Irish Sea to deal with this very infrequent problem'.[1] In effect, McClure gave the Northern Irish government's decision medical benefaction because he believed that the current legal situation correctly rested the power in medical hands.

A few months previously, McClure, a man of considerable medical experience who had worked in obstetrics and gynaecology in Northern Ireland since 1932,[2] outlined the rationale for resisting the extension of

[1] *Hansard N.I. (Commons)*, vol. lxxi, 1968, 69, col. 505. Cited in Benson, 'The Provision of Abortion in Northern Ireland, 1900–1968', pp. 29–30.

[2] His obituary notes that McClure was a deeply religious Christian, although his denomination is not noted. H. Ian McClure, 'Obituary', *British Medical Journal*, 284 (March 1982), p. 906.

the 1967 act to his medical colleagues.[3] This speech offers history one of the few explanations of why this momentous piece of legislation was not extended to Northern Ireland. In essence, McClure argued that it was better for Northern Irish abortions to continue to be governed by 'statute and case law', because of the unique religious sensibilities and history of the region. He reiterated the salient parts of the Roman Catholic encyclical *Casti Connubii*, which deemed that the life of mother and foetus were 'equally sacred' and consequently, 'no one has the power, not even the public authority, to destroy it'.[4] However, he pointed out, the 1938 Bourne case had also established that, while it was not legal to perform an abortion just because a woman wanted one, nor was it legal to refuse to perform one for 'religious reasons', when a woman's health required it.[5] The implication was that without the protection of case law, Catholic teaching might have prevented Catholic doctors from performing therapeutic abortions and Catholic women from availing of them.

McClure believed the *status quo* would serve Northern Ireland better because it allowed Northern Irish doctors, on a case-by-case basis, acting in 'good faith', to decide when an abortion was necessary and legal. The idea of 'good faith', he reminded his audience, had been established by the 1938 Bourne case and reinforced in the 1958 Regina v. Newton and Stungo case. In the latter case, the judge explained that abortions should be carried out 'in good faith for the purposes of preserving the life or health of the woman, and when I say health I mean not only her physical health but also her mental health'.[6] Perhaps constrained by the fragility of the denominational entente in medical practice in Northern Ireland, McClure did not spell out his meaning, but by juxtaposing Catholic teaching and case law on therapeutic abortion, he was underscoring that the latter allowed doctors acting in 'good faith' to protect the women of Northern Ireland from unnecessary death or harm as a result of pregnancy. In his view, the middle-ground in religious and moral terms was already secured in relation to abortion in Northern Ireland: women could not dictate the terms of an abortion and nor could the Roman

[3]This was then published, see, H. Ian McClure, 'The Law and Therapeutic Abortion', *Ulster Medical Journal*, 36:2 (1967), pp. 111–17.

[4]Ibid.

[5]Ibid.

[6]Ibid., p. 112. For a good review of the importance of this case, M. P. Clark, *Legal Medicine in History* (Cambridge: Cambridge University Press), pp. 335–37.

Catholic authorities or any doctor's religious views. As Michael Clark observed: 'The effect of these legal developments was to prevent the ethical question abortion raised from being answered by women themselves; it was placed firmly in doctor's hands'.[7] This is precisely what appealed to McClure and the establishment in Northern Ireland.

While the religious denominations in Northern Ireland were all inherently conservative on the issue of abortion, there were differences of degree and, as the history of birth control in the province demonstrated, these required careful balancing and some ambiguity to keep everyone on side or at least quiet. McClure feared that a change in the *status quo* would jeopardise this equilibrium. The Medical Termination of Pregnáncy Bill (as the abortion bill of 1967 was known) thus posed:

> the obvious danger on the one hand of opening the legal door too widely and so increasing present abuses, and on the other of framing the law too closely on the question of indications for such must be sufficiently flexible to keep advancement of medical science.[8]

McClure therefore contended that the current situation was sufficiently clear and flexible to allow doctors to decide the medical basis of abortions in Northern Ireland. A new law risked being both vague enough to allow women rather than doctors to decide the terms of abortions *and* too precise in its definitions, potentially limiting doctors' medical room for manoeuvre in line with scientific advancements. Crucially, for McClure, the proposed British abortion legislation ran the risk of taking the decision out of doctors' hands and, thereby, disrupting the *modus operandi* in Northern Ireland, which allowed doctors, guided by the principles of good faith and existing legal constraints, to judge when an abortion was appropriate.

It is clear that McClure and his rationale were instrumental in providing the grounds to prevent the extension of the British Abortion Act in 1967. It could best be described as a policy of 'let sleeping dogs lie'. The Attorney General's apparently innocuous declaration in January 1969 that the 1967 Abortion Act could not be extended to Northern Ireland due to the 'feelings' of the people, therefore masked a complex history of negotiation, compromise and nuance, which underpinned the

[7] Clark, *Legal Medicine in History*, p. 337.

[8] McClure, 'The Law and Therapeutic Abortion', p. 114.

practice of medicine in a fraught political and religious context. McClure provides a rare glimpse of the dynamics of power and its subtle negotiation in Northern Ireland. This incident typified the way in which these sensitive issues were dealt with in the province: behind closed doors with the express intention of drawing as little attention as desirable in order to keep power in as few hands as possible. The implications were to be incalculable.

Amending the Republic: 1983

In the Republic of Ireland, the 1980s represented a battle ground between the forces first delineated during the campaign for the legalisation of contraception.[9] Conservatives in the Republic regarded family planning legislation as a breach of Ireland's moral *cordon sanitaire* and were determined to prevent any further 'erosion'. These conservative forces were largely Catholics over the age of thirty-five and drawn from rural Ireland, and were increasingly represented by Fianna Fáil.[10] The Catholic Church was at the vanguard, in particular Bishop Kevin McNamara, who argued that the Irish family was under attack from the corrosive effects of the 'contraceptive mentality', which resulted in the failure of marriages and recourse to abortion.[11] These groups were instrumental in spearheading a campaign to ensure that abortion would not be legalised in Ireland. As Tom Hesketh has remarked, their pro-life stand was 'anticipative', because unlike in Britain and America, there

[9]This is generally accepted view in the historiography, see: M. J. Maguire, 'The Changing Face of Catholic Ireland: Conservatism and Liberalism in the Ann Lovett and Kerry Babies Scandals', *Feminist Studies*, 27:2 (Summer 2001), pp. 335–58; S. McAvoy, 'From Anti-Amendment Campaigns to Demanding Reproductive Justice: The Changing Landscape of Abortion Rights Activism in Ireland, 1983–2008' in Schweppe, *The Unborn Child, Article 40.3.3 and Abortion in Ireland*, pp. 15–47.

[10]B. Girvin, 'An Irish Solution to an Irish Problem: Catholicism, Contraception and Change, 1922–1979', *Contemporary European History*, 27:1 (2018), pp. 1–22, p. 9.

[11]Bishop Kevin McNamara, *The Family Today* (Dublin: Irish Messenger, 1984), p. 7. K. McNamara served as bishop of Kerry between 1976 and 1984, where he became a vocal defender of Catholic family values. His reputation in that regard may well have influenced the Vatican in appointing him archbishop of Dublin in 1985, where he remained until his death in 1987. See, D. C. Sheehy, 'McNamara, Kevin', in J. McGuire and J. Quinn, (eds), *Dictionary of Irish Biography*, http://dib.cambridge.org.ucd.idm.oclc.org/quicksearch.do#.

were no pro-choice campaigns in Ireland and no talk of overturning the 1861 ban enshrined in the Offences Against the Person Act.[12] Feminism was clearly in the sights of this conservative backlash as it had been since universal suffrage was mooted in the early 1900s, when the Catholic Church argued it would undermine the family and women's position in society.[13] These old arguments were once again recycled.

These conservative arguments were met with a rapidly developing narrative of privacy, which emphasised the role of personal conscience and the idea of women's and civil rights.[14] However, that is not to imply that any section of Irish society embraced abortion, rather the dilemmas abortion raised went to the heart of this more nuanced understanding of personal autonomy, rights and responsibilities. Much of this agenda was driven by a new generation of educated men and women, many of them journalists and influential professionals, often represented by Labour and Fine Gael parties. There was also evidence of more diffuse change. A sociological study of small farms in the West of Ireland in 1977 claimed that the influence of 'modernisation' in relation to higher levels of education, social and geographic mobility, and exposure to media (half of the houses had a television and all had a radio) 'appeared to be changing people's values'. It concluded that one-quarter to one-third of households appeared to 'be closer to the "modern" urban middle-class model of family interaction i.e. low sex segregation in task roles, high jointness in task and decision-making roles'.[15] Another study of the same year, noted significant changes in relation to people's moral judgements:

[12] T. Hesketh, *The Second Partitioning of Ireland? The Abortion Referendum of 1983* (Dublin: Brandsma Books, 1990), p. 2.

[13] For a classic presentation of this case see, D. Barry, 'Female Suffrage from a Catholic Standpoint', *Irish Ecclesiastical Record*, 26 (September 1909), pp. 295–303. The same argument was recycled again in relation to women working outside the home, see Rev. C. Lucey, 'The Problem of the Woman Worker', *Irish Ecclesiastical Record*, 48 (July–December 1936), pp. 449–67.

[14] McAvoy, 'From Anti-Amendment Campaigns to Demanding Reproductive Justice', pp. 15–47.

[15] D. F. Hannan and L. A. Katsiaouni, *Traditional Families? From Culturally Prescribed to Negotiated Roles in Farm Families* (Dublin: The Economic and Social Research Institute, 1977), pp. 5, 11.

'There has been a unanimous response (98.6 per cent) in favour of the same treatment for ***children born out of wedlock*** as those in marriage'.[16]

In April 1981, the 'Pro-Life Amendment Campaign' [hereafter PLAC] was launched to enshrine protection for the unborn in the Irish constitution.[17] The campaign sought to keep the debate focused on the fundamental rights of the unborn and *away* from women's health or rights to marital privacy, precisely because it feared such arguments might open the gate to abortion.[18] As Morgan Healey argues, in this pro-life mentality, abortion symbolised the perceived threat to 'an exceptional form of Irish Catholic morality' (Fig. 5.1).[19] However, this ideological view ignored the reality of thousands of Irish women seeking abortions in Britain, and the very real risks that pregnancy posed to some women's health. Fundamental to this view was a denial of any feminist arguments in favour of abortion as a reproductive right.[20] Indeed, as noted, feminism was seen as central to the 'problem'. The idea of choice had little resonance. As Linda Connolly argues, this also pertained on the anti-amendment side which for strategic reasons 'silenced' the issue of women's reproductive rights.[21] This, she argues, was facilitated in part by the fact that few women's organisations 'confronted the Irish abortion rate *systematically* as a feminist issue', with the exception of the IWU and Women's Right to Choose group.[22]

[16] M. MacGréil, *Prejudice and Tolerance in Ireland* (Dublin: College of Industrial Relations, 1977), p. 410.

[17] It was established with members of the Catholic Doctors' Guild, representatives of the Council of Special Concern and of the Irish Branch of a British organisation, the Responsible Society, at its core. Society for the Protection of Unborn Children [SPUC] also entered the fold at its launch. McAvoy, 'From Anti-Amendment Campaigns to Demanding Reproductive Justice', p. 23.

[18] Schweppe, 'Introduction', in Schweppe, *The Unborn Child, Article 40.3.3 and Abortion in Ireland,* pp. 1–14, p. 4; S. Mullally, 'Abortion Law: Rights Discourse, Dissent and Reproductive Autonomy', ibid., pp. 213–45, p. 220.

[19] M. Healey, '"I Don't Want to Get into This, It's Too Controversial": How Irish Women Politicians Conceptualise the Abortion Debate' in Schweppe, *The Unborn Child, Article 40.3.3 and Abortion in Ireland*, pp. 65–85, p. 67.

[20] On feminist action with regard to abortion in the 1980s, see. Connolly, *The Irish Women's Movement*, pp. 155–86.

[21] Ibid., p. 164.

[22] Ibid., p. 160. Connolly's emphasis.

Fig. 5.1 Pro-life march in favour of the eighth amendment to the Irish Constitution, Dublin, 27 December 1982. Photo by Derek Speirs

Thus, while those in favour of the amendment could muster a focused and fundamentalist campaign, those opposed to it had much more multifaceted concerns incorporating both those in favour of some form of abortion in Ireland and those in vehement opposition. For example, the Anti-Amendment Campaign [AAC] had five main concerns: abortion was an issue best handled by legislation; the amendment would cause medical and legal confusion and threaten women's lives; it did not deal with the ever-increasing numbers of Irish women travelling for abortions; energy should instead be focused on improving conditions for unmarried mothers and their children and, finally, the amendment was sectarian, opposed by the main Protestant and Jewish faiths.[23]

The campaign that ensued is still remembered by many for its viciousness, referred to by the *Irish Times* as 'the second partitioning of Ireland'. Indeed, the same editorial presciently warned: 'if this amendment goes through, there will be legal arguments forever, and civil war among the doctors, especially the paediatricians and gynaecologists'.[24] During the campaign, the more extreme elements cast abortion as a colonial wrongdoing, declaring: 'The abortion Mills of England grind Irish Babies into Blood that Cries out to Heaven for Vengeance' and 'Abortion is a wrong that the English do to the Irish'.[25] While there was a broad range of arguments on both sides of the debate, it essentially came down to whether or not the constitution was the place for a prohibition on abortion and whether the wording would have the desired effect or if it would, in fact, increase the risks pregnancy posed to mothers by inhibiting doctors' ability to protect her health and, ultimately, her life. Some of the first organisations to express opposition to the idea of such a referendum were the Well Woman Centres, the Irish Family Planning Associations, the Council for the Status of Women [hereafter CSW] and the Irish Council for Civil Liberties. Many women's organisations also mobilised around the AAC, for example, the Irish Pregnancy Counselling Centre [hereafter IPPC], the Women's Right to Choose group, and the Irish Women's Abortion Support group [hereafter IWASG] in London.[26] Criticism from the Workers' Party, the Chairman of the Labour Party and Senator Mary Robinson, also of Labour, marked the beginnings of an influential left-wing coalition against the amendment.[27] By the end of the campaign only Fianna Fáil remained behind the PLAC campaign, while divisions had emerged

[23] See Healey, 'I Don't Want to Get into This, It's Too Controversial'.

[24] 'The Second Partitioning of Ireland', *Irish Times*, 30 August 1983; Hesketh gives this as the reason for the title of his book on the referendum. See, Hesketh, *The Second Partitioning of Ireland?* p. 75.

[25] R. Fletcher, 'Post-colonial Fragments: Representations of Abortion in Irish Law and Politics', *Journal of Law and Society*, 28:4 (December 2001), p. 577.

[26] This list was sourced from Connolly, *The Irish Women's Movement*, p. 158.

[27] Hesketh, *The Second Partitioning of Ireland?* pp. 58–59.

in Fine Gael and Labour, with prominent members of the latter very vocal in opposing the amendment.[28]

As with birth control, it was Fianna Fáil's Charles Haughey, this time as Taoiseach, who oversaw the crafting of the amendment, which was published in November 1982 (just before his government fell) to a lukewarm reception from those in favour *and* those opposed to the idea of an amendment. The amendment read: 'The State acknowledges the right to life of the unborn and, with due regard to the equal right to life of the mother, guarantees in its laws to respect, and, as far as practicable, by its laws to defend and vindicate that right'.[29] The danger of this wording was amply highlighted; the Attorney General, Peter Sutherland warned in February 1983 that it could prevent doctors from intervening in cases where pregnancy threatened the life of the woman, since they would be required to show equal regard for the life of the unborn.[30] A mother from Limerick wrote to *Woman's Way* in July 1983 to explain her reservations:

> I am totally against the proposed wording of the amendment to the constitution and naturally will not be voting in favour of it although I detest abortion on demand and I am a mother of twelve...What I strongly object to is giving the foetus equal rights to the mother. During pregnancy the mother can develop complications requiring medical help which may result in terminating the life of the foetus.

Thus, she believed that doctors should be free to give advice as 'a mother's life is so precious in procreating and rearing her children that the best medical skill should always be used to protect her life'.[31]

The issue of maternal health was brought into sharp focus on 2 September, a few days before the referendum, when journalist Pádraig Yeates informed the Irish public about the death of Sheila Hodgers. He told this story as an example of what the eighth amendment might mean for sick pregnant women. Mrs. Hodgers, a mother of two, had her cancer treatment withdrawn by Our Lady of Lourdes Hospital in Drogheda, a private Catholic hospital, because she was pregnant. On Saint Patrick's

[28] Ibid., pp. 113–44.

[29] It is currently Article 40.3.3 of the Irish Constitution.

[30] 'Attorney General Rules Out Wording', *Irish Times*, 16 February 1983.

[31] 'What You Say', *Woman's Way* (1 July 1983), p. 5

Day 1983, she gave birth in 'agony' to a daughter who died immediately; she died several days later.[32] Yeates pointed out that this case had deliberately been withheld from the referendum debate:

> Despite the ramifications of the case and the fact that it is known to many members of the medical profession, it has never been raised during the current debate. Nor have other "hard" cases which reveal defects, not alone in the thinking behind the amendment, but in the prevailing medical ethics of many of our hospitals. The reason, as one of the consultants concerned put it bluntly, is fear. To talk about individual cases like that of Sheila Hodgers was, he admitted, "more than my livelihood is worth."[33]

In other words, Yeates highlighted how vulnerable all pregnant women in Ireland were under the 1861 act, which made no provisions relating to their protection, and how the 1983 referendum would further restrict doctor's room for legal manoeuvre. Yeates's piece, of course, begged the questions: How many other 'hard cases' had been kept from the public over the years? How many justifiable therapeutic abortions had been denied to Irish women?

The publication of Sheila Hodgers's story did not sway public opinion. The Republic of Ireland's constitutional referendum was held on 7 September 1983 and the people voted to insert the eighth amendment into the constitution by a majority of 841,233 (66.9%) to 416,136 (33.10%).[34] The turnout of 53.67 was low. As Máire Nic Ghiolla Phadraig observed: 'after a prolonged debate only half the electorate turned out to vote and one-third of these voted against the amendment'.[35] Despite this, some boldly interpreted this as a rebellion 'against the abortion cult which has swept across the world'.[36]

The 1983 campaign engaged almost all sectors of society, providing a platform for a host of anxieties about how Ireland was 'modernising',

[32] P. Yeates, 'Sheila Hodgers—A Case in Question', *Irish Times*, 2 September 1983. For a review of this case see, F. O'Toole, 'The Ugly Politics of the Womb', *Irish Times*, 5 August 2003.

[33] Yeates, 'Sheila Hodgers—A Case in Question'.

[34] https://electionsireland.org/results/referendum/refdetail.cfm?ref=1983R, accessed 19 March 2018.

[35] M. Nic Ghiolla Phádraig, 'Social and Cultural Factors in Family Planning', *The Changing Family* (Family Studies Unit, UCD, 1984), pp. 58–97, p. 80.

[36] *Fermanagh Herald*, 29 February 1992, p. 12.

about the role of the state, women, sexuality and the place of religion. It had also allowed space for people to highlight the reality of Ireland's 'hidden' abortion trail. By the mid-1980s, there was an established narrative in the more liberal sections of the Irish press about Ireland's hypocritical response to abortion which was 'pushed out of sight on the Liverpool boat'.[37] Then, on the afternoon of the 31 January 1984, the bodies of a fifteen-year-old schoolgirl Ann Lovett and her new-born infant were discovered in Granard, Co. Longford, under a statue of the Virgin Mary. The death of this schoolgirl and her baby of exposure seemed to underscore this sense of national duplicity. Ireland was a society in which a young girl clearly felt she could not seek help with her pregnancy. That she gave birth in church grounds under a religious statue of the most important mother in Catholic theology seemed to symbolise the price Irish women had paid for society's moral hypocrisy. The Minister for Women's Affairs lamented: 'There is little indication that a caring society has emerged fully in the wake of the three-year pro-life debate we have just gone through'.[38] Only a few months later the country was plunged into another controversy, which exposed the vulnerability of all women in Ireland, with the arrest of Joanne Hayes for the murder of two new-born infants whose bodies were found in Co. Kerry. Ms. Hayes had given birth to one of these infants, it was buried on her family's farm, but the other was found on a beach eighty kilometres away from her home. The charges against her were eventually dropped and a tribunal of inquiry was held in Tralee, Co. Kerry, into the police's handling of the case. However, many contemporaries regarded this tribunal as a pretext to effectively put Joanne Hayes on trial. During the tribunal her moral character was questioned and details of her sex life and menstrual cycle were pored over. At times she was so upset she was sedated in order to continue to give evidence and years later, the journalist and feminist, Nell McCafferty, recalled the horror of it all: 'we heard her [Joanne Hayes] out in the corridor retching and crying. She was brought in sedated, so heavily sedated that her head kept bobbing off the microphone'.[39] It was a display of misogyny writ large. Writing

[37] M. Holland, 'An Issue the Liverpool Boat Can't Carry Away', *Irish Times*, 25 June 1986.

[38] R. Holohan, 'Girl and Baby Death Inquiry to Be Private', *Irish Times*, 7 February 1984.

[39] For Nell McCafferty's recollections see, https://radio.rte.ie/radio1highlights/kerry-babies-drivetime/. The Irish state finally apologized to Joanne Hayes in January 2018. For a detailed contemporary account of how she was treated see, McCafferty, *A Woman to Blame*.

at the time, McCafferty remarked: 'There is a sense...of womanhood itself being on trial here, and the traumatic echoes of the amendment debate...about sex and wombs and blood and babies done to death'. The country, she concluded, needed reminding that this was 'Tralee, not Iran', driving home a sense that Ireland was an outlier in terms of Western European values.[40]

There were outpourings of grief for Ann Lovett and support for Joanne Hayes. People, particularly women, travelled from all over Ireland to stand outside the Kerry Babies' Tribunal in solidarity with Joanne Hayes. One banner held by a woman read: 'Joanne is a victim not a criminal',[41] encapsulating a narrative that was to grow in the proceeding years: in Ireland it was often women who were criminalised for the crimes of men. Significantly, a study of values and attitudes on the island in 1984 observed that 'Ireland remains an outstandingly religious country'. However, it confirmed shifting ground as 'only a third of respondents believed that their church's answers were adequate on moral problems and problems of family life'.[42] After years of debate on the issue, the survey found that, although the overall attitude to abortion was negative, the majority of those under forty-five years of age believed that abortion was 'justified on grounds of the mother's health'.[43] The pro-life amendment campaign had stirred up as much as it had settled.

Research carried out by the Irish Consumer Research group in the mid-1980s into Irish housewives produced yet more insights into the complex world of Irish values.[44] It found 'a nostalgia for the idea

[40] N. McCafferty, 'Womanhood Goes on Trial in Tralee', *Irish Press*, 16 January 1985.

[41] This banner is depicted in a photograph taken by Michael MacSweeny, which featured in an article by D. Ferriter, 'Detective Gerry O'Carroll Owes Joanne Hayes an Apology', *Irish Times*, 20 January 2018, https://www.irishtimes.com/opinion/detective-gerry-o-carroll-owes-joanne-hayes-an-apology-1.3360692, accessed 1 September 2018.

[42] M. Fogarty, L. Ryan, and J. Lee (eds), *Irish Values and Attitudes: The Irish Report of the European Value Systems Study* (Dublin: Dominican Publications, 1984), pp. 8, 99.

[43] Ibid., p. 47.

[44] This survey defined housewives as women who were mainly responsible for the running of a household, but who might also work full or part-time outside that household. It put the number of housewives in Ireland at 845,000, which translated into a third of the adult population and two-thirds of the adult female population. L. Collins, *The Irish Housewife—A Portrait* (Dublin: Irish Consumer Research, 1986), pp. 3–5.

of the very large families', but a 'fairly general feeling amongst housewives that contraception within marriage is now an acceptable and desirable thing'.[45] While 'abortion is more widely looked upon with aversion, there are some younger housewives, especially in urban areas, who visualize situations where abortion might be justified. Such cases might include the woman who had been a victim of rape, or whose life was in danger because of her pregnancy'.[46] As a Co. Offaly wife in her late forties explained: 'I do think a mother who is seriously ill – wouldn't it be terrible to let her die rather than to have an abortion?'[47]

Abortion and the Courts

There was, however, movement afoot to make these journeys to Britain for abortions more hazardous and secretive. In January 1987, Justice Liam Hamilton granted the Society for Protection of the Unborn Child [hereafter SPUC], a central player in the PLAC group, an injunction against the only two clinics offering non-directive pregnancy counselling, including abortion information, in the Republic: the Open Door Counselling and Dublin Well Woman Centre.[48] Hamilton ruled that the right to life of the unborn was a 'fundamental right' that superseded the right to information regarding abortion in Britain. In 1988 the Irish Supreme Court confirmed Hamilton's ruling, in fact, it extended the existing criminal law to make it an offence for professional service providers to give practical information to women seeking legal abortions abroad. The Supreme Court ruled that service providers be 'perpetually restrained from assisting pregnant women within the jurisdiction to travel abroad to obtain abortions by referral to a clinic, by the making for them of travel arrangements'.[49]

This ruling did not, of course, stop the outflow of women; it merely made it more frightening, stressful and dangerous. It was no longer

[45] Ibid., p. 64.

[46] Ibid., p. 69.

[47] Ibid., p. 75.

[48] U. Barry, 'Abortion in Ireland', *Feminist Review*, 29 (1988), pp. 57–66.

[49] Cited in Connolly, *The Irish Women's Movement*, p. 171.

possible for women to be referred from one medical system to another; women now had to make that transition themselves in an information void. It is hard to overstate the devastating impact of this information blackout. The ruling left women, counsellors, doctors and those concerned with women's reproductive health, fearful. Those wishing to support women seeking abortions, and this baton was largely taken up by other women, were forced to rely on a secret underground network and adopt code names.[50] As a temporary measure, the founder of Open Door Counselling, Ruth Riddick used her own phone number to continue non-directive counselling from her home.[51] British magazines appeared on the Irish market with the pages containing abortion information blacked out. In the public toilets around Ireland, telephone numbers for abortion clinics were scribbled in resistance, but this was no compensation for proper channels of information and support. The fear was intermingled with trauma and many women from across the island simply buried their experiences, never seeking counselling or even the solace of conversation after a termination. The SPUC ruling also delayed abortion travel: 'one British service in Liverpool reported a 57 per cent increase in Irish women seeking an abortion after 15 weeks, resulting from their difficulty in getting basic information at home'.[52]

Linda Connolly notes that women's groups refocused their energies from campaigning for the right to choose to working to protect Irish women's right to procure abortion outside the state. For example, the Women's Right to Choose group was replaced in 1987 by the Women's Information Network [hereafter WIN] in Dublin. WIN was an underground organisation, which sought to provide non-directive information to women facing crisis pregnancies. Connolly astutely observes that this aim was more acceptable to the mainstream women's movement and the general public.[53] Ann Rossiter's oral history of London-Irish

[50] A. Rossiter, *Ireland's Hidden Diaspora: The 'Abortion Trail' and the Making of a London-Irish Underground, 1980–2000* (London: Iasc, 2009), p. 96; Connolly, *The Irish Women's Movement*, p. 174.

[51] This was to replace Open Door Counselling and was known as Open Line telephone helpline and continued for many years. Connolly, *The Irish Women's Movement*, p. 170.

[52] M. Maher, '1,850 Irishwomen Travel to Britain for Abortion', *Irish Times*, 19 January 1988.

[53] Connolly, *The Irish Women's Movement*, p. 175.

women who worked during the 1980s and 1990s similarly highlights the importance of these groups in circumventing Irish censorship.[54] Rossiter herself was a member of the IWASG, one of the key British-based support groups. The work of women in Britain, mainly though not exclusively Irish or of Irish descent, is a vital part of the Irish abortion story and one that underscores the significance of female networks across borders. Kate Duke, who also worked with the IWASG in London in the 1980s, recalled that during this period: 'I do remember vividly while answering the phone…women whispering'.[55] Women were literally afraid to be heard uttering the word abortion. IWASG and other groups, such as the Irish Abortion Solidarity Campaign [hereafter IASC], did not just offer vital and practical support to Irish women seeking abortions, they fund raised for organisations in Ireland and campaigned for a change to Irish law. As Rossiter observes, the activity of these networks was often underground and, such was the atmosphere of fear, that the IWASG used a code name 'Imelda' so that women could talk openly without mentioning the word abortion.[56]

Between 1988 and 2002, despite growing evidence of the distress the censorship of abortion information was causing and the knowledge that it was having *no* impact on the numbers travelling for terminations, the Irish state persistently attempted to keep this information from women and even contemplated preventing women leaving the state for abortions. In 1991, in a bid to guarantee that the European Community would not interfere on the issue, the Irish government entered a protocol to the Maastricht Treaty to ensure that European decisions would not 'affect the application in Ireland of Article 40.3.3' referring to the right to the life of the unborn.[57] In 1992, the Irish High Court granted an injunction against a fourteen-year-old rape victim to prevent her leaving Ireland to have an abortion in England. Suddenly, the journey, which an estimated twelve Irish women a day were making, was thrown into the spotlight. This became known as the 'X' case, to protect the identity of the girl at the centre of the story. It is widely regarded as having changed the narrative on abortion in Ireland. As Lisa Smyth argues,

[54] For a detailed analysis of these groups see, Rossiter, *Ireland's Hidden Diaspora*.

[55] Rossiter, *Ireland's Hidden Diaspora*, p. 97.

[56] Ibid., p. 96.

[57] McAvoy, 'From Anti-Amendment campaigns to Demanding Reproductive Justice', p. 30.

'the degree of state control over women, through control over women's bodies, became suddenly visible through the X case'.[58] The case raised such basic questions: did Irish women have the right to travel? How far could the state go, or was willing to go, in its attempts to stop women making fundamental decisions about their bodies and reproductive health? Would the Irish people tolerate a raped child being held in the state against her will to prevent her ending a pregnancy forced upon her? Adding further fuel to the sense of outrage that year was the European Court of Human Rights ruling on the Open Door Counselling appeal of the 1987 Hamilton ruling. The European Court concluded that the Irish courts were in breach of the Human Right's Convention's information right's clause, which guaranteed the right 'to receive and impart information and ideas without interference by public authority and without frontiers'.[59]

In her analysis of the 1992 X case, Mary Muldowney stresses the depth of public outrage and the general dismay and shame that a child was being victimised by a constitutional amendment sold to protect children. She also notes that this case underscored the complexity of individual abortion stories and how punitive the Irish response had been in reality.[60] This sense, articulated during the Kerry Babies' Tribunal, that Ireland penalised women for the crimes of men was captured by a banner, held at one of the large public protest marches in support of the girl at the centre of the case, which read: 'Ireland defends men's right to procreate by rape'.[61] The mood was one of rage and a sense of gender discrimination was central to it, for example, posters carried at the various marches decried 'Ireland's iron curtain', 'Women's rights RIP – 1992',

[58] L. Smyth, 'Narratives of Irishness and the Problem of Abortion: The X Case 1992', *Feminist Review*, 60 (1998), pp. 61–83. See ATTORNEY GENERAL Plaintiff v. X. and OTHERS Defendants [1992 No. 846 P], found at http://www.supremecourt.ie/supremecourt/sclibrary3.nsf/0/9FA0AA8E8D261FC48025765C0042F6B3?openDocument&l=en.

[59] Cited in Connolly, *The Irish Women's Movement*, p. 177.

[60] M. Muldowney, 'Breaking the Silence: Pro-choice Activism in Ireland Since 1983', in J. Redmond, S. Tiernan, S. McAvoy, and M. McAuliffe (eds), *Sexual Politics in Modern Ireland* (Dublin: Irish Academic Press, 2015), pp. 127–50, p. 134.

[61] This poster appears in photographs taken by Derek Speirs of the 17 February 1992 march in Dublin.

Fig. 5.2 Public demonstration following the 1992 X case, Dublin, 25 February 1992. Photo by Derek Speirs

'Licence to rape'[62] and 'Scrape the Amendment! No Internment of Women' (Fig. 5.2).[63] Amid this uproar, the Supreme Court overturned the injunction on the basis that the risk of suicide represented 'a real and substantial risk to the life, as distinct from the health, of the mother, which can only be avoided by the termination of her pregnancy, such termination is permissible'. This ruling effectively meant abortion, when suicide was a risk, was now legal in the Republic of Ireland. However, as Louise Ryan highlights, it also 'demonstrated that Irish official policy on unwanted pregnancy could only work, and had ever only worked,

[62] These posters appear in photographs taken by Derek Speirs at a Dublin march on 22 February 1992.

[63] This poster appears in photographs taken by Derek Speirs of the 25 February 1992 march in Dublin.

because women availed of services outside the state'.[64] Indeed, in 1992 the government put three referendums to the people, two of which were passed: one, the thirteenth amendment to the Irish constitution, which safeguarded the right to travel and another, the fourteenth amendment, which effectively reversed the ban on the right to information relating to abortions outside the state. In other words, the Irish people voted to continue to allow women to leave the state to terminate pregnancies and to ensure their entitlement to information regarding those services. Remarkably, given the public outpouring, the third referendum, the twelfth amendment to the Irish constitution, would have nullified the implications of the Supreme Court's ruling in the X case. The wording specified that the health of the mother, even the 'risk of self-destruction', was not sufficient grounds for a legal termination.[65] The Irish people rejected this attempt to prioritise the rights of the unborn over the health, including mental health, of pregnant women but no legislation respecting this result followed. In fact, after the government again attempted and failed to row back on the X case ruling via a referendum in 2002, Fianna Fáil's Bertie Ahern, the then Taoiseach, declared he would neither hold another referendum on the issue and or legislate according to the people's vote.[66]

A Moral Alliance: Northern Ireland and Abortion

Somewhat disingenuously, following the 1992 Supreme Court ruling in the X case, the *Ulster Herald* declared this a 'solution which at best amounts to abortion by export and more likely this will amount to abortion services being provided by this State'.[67] In actual fact, Northern Ireland had proved just as adept as the Republic of Ireland at exporting abortion. In 1983, prompted by the referendum in the Republic, the British Medical Association had recommended extending the 1967

[64] L. Ryan, '"A Decent Girl Well Worth Helping": Women, Migration and Unwanted Pregnancy', in L. Harte and Y. Whelan (eds), *Ireland Beyond Boundaries: Mapping Irish Studies in the Twenty-First Century* (Dublin: Pluto Press, 2007), pp. 135–53, p. 152.

[65] Referendum (Amendment) (no. 2) Act, 1992, http://www.irishstatutebook.ie/eli/1992/act/22/enacted/en/html.

[66] B. Ahern with R. Aldous, *Bertie Ahern: The Autobiography* (Dublin: Arrow, 2010), p. 252.

[67] *Ulster Herald*, 9 May 1992.

Abortion Act to Northern Ireland, pointing out that 'abortion was illegal in the North, women had to travel to Liverpool for operations'.[68] This clarification was necessary because the fact that the 1967 act had not been extended to Northern Ireland was not widely known, nor was the fact that Northern Irish women had to pay, just like their southern Irish counterparts, for their abortions on the NHS. However, as the *Irish Times'* religious correspondent noted: 'In Northern Ireland there is widescale ecumenical co-operation in relation to abortion. Protestants and Roman Catholics co-operate in complete harmony in [the] Life [organisation], a body which opposes abortion on "moral grounds"'. Indeed, Life declared that there 'is no issue on which the people of Ireland are more united than in their opposition to the destruction of the life of the unborn child'.[69]

Abortion was only available in Northern Ireland in very strict medical circumstances and a remarkably similar tone of shame and moral judgement surrounded the subject across the island until at least the 1990s. Morally conservative sections of the Northern Irish press put the increasing numbers of women from Ireland having abortions in Britain down to 'widespread moral confusion' and warned those who counselled and advised those women 'bear as great, if not a greater degree of guilt than the girls and women themselves'.[70] Practitioners in Britain who provided Northern Irishwomen with abortions were also deemed to be involved in an 'evil practice'.[71] In 1991, little had changed in conservative views; the Bishop of Raphoe, the Most Rev. Séamus Hegarty, proclaimed that those who 'knowingly procured' an abortion were 'accomplices to murder' who had 'sinned and broken God's law'.[72] As a 1999 *Guardian* article observed: 'abortion is such an emotive issue that it unites fundamentalists on both sides of the religious divide'.[73] Pauline O'Hara, who had accompanied a friend seeking an abortion during this period, framed her sense of fear upon returning to Northern Ireland in

[68] Dr. Tom McKinstry is cited while attending the BMA annual meeting, see, *Irish Times*, 1 July 1983.

[69] P. Nolan, 'Consistent Christian Opposition to Abortion', *Irish Times*, 15 February 1983.

[70] *Ulster Herald*, 10 May 1975.

[71] *Fermanagh Herald*, 14 May 1988.

[72] 'Abortion a Grievous Sin', *Ulster Herald*, 19 October 1991, front page.

[73] 'The Other Troubles', *The Guardian*, 17 August 1999.

terms remarkably similar to her southern counterparts: 'I accompanied her to Liverpool and I remember that we were very frightened with the whole business of going to England in such circumstances...When we returned to Belfast I realised that abortion was such a taboo subject that my friend just wanted to put it behind her and we never spoke of it again'. This experience motivated O'Hara to join the Northern Ireland Law Reform Association [hereafter NILRA], one of the organisations in Northern Ireland fighting for the reform of abortion laws in the province.[74]

Despite the legal risks, it was women in Northern Ireland who responded to the evident needs of other women in providing support and advice and thus continued a practice long evident in both states. The Ulster Pregnancy Information Service, later known as the Ulster Pregnancy Advisory Association [hereafter UPAA], for example, estimated that from 1971 to 1999 it counselled 1000 women per annum, comprising half of all women who travelled from Northern Ireland for an abortion.[75] Seeing women of all denominations, including small numbers from the Republic of Ireland, the organisation quickly realised that women were too 'humiliated and distressed' for information to suffice. These women needed 'moral support...as few felt able to cope in the face of a complicated personal situation, the raising of a sum of money quickly, and the ordeal of a journey "across the sea"'.[76] Indicative of the risks these women ran, and continue to run, were the constant protests outside its tiny Belfast office, which was eventually attacked by arsonists forcing the UPAA to close its doors in August 1999. The fate of one of the few services willing to offer advice to women with unwanted pregnancies is illustrative of the depth of hostility to reproductive rights, the antipathy of wider society and the complicity of the polity.

The Northern Irish political response to the abortion issue amounted to little more than continuous efforts to prevent the extension of the 1967 Abortion Act. This was, of course, only possible because of an uncharacteristic cross-party unity *and* successive British governments'

[74] Cited in Rossiter, *Ireland's Hidden Diaspora*, p. 147.

[75] McCormick, 'No Sense of Wrongdoing', p. 141. Lorna Goldstrom and her husband founded this organisation. 'Obituary: Max Goldstrom: Social and Economic Historian', *The Sunday Times*, 19 August 2009.

[76] P. A. Compton, L. Goldstrom, and J. M. C. Goldstrom, 'Religion and Legal Abortion in Northern Ireland', *Journal of Biosocial Science*, 6 (1974), p. 495.

willingness to facilitate the situation.[77] In 2007, the Democratic Unionist Party's Tom Buchanan depicted the 1967 legislation as 'a most ungodly Act that legislated for the murder of the unborn child'.[78] Sinn Fein's group leader in the Northern Ireland Assembly, John O'Dowd concurred: 'Sinn Féin, despite some propaganda to the contrary, does not support abortion. The simple fact is that it does not support the Abortion Act 1967 being introduced here'.[79] In consequence, even during the fraught peace negotiations of the late 1990s, a deal was done with Northern Irish political parties to prevent the extension of the 1967 act to Northern Ireland. Just as in 1967, this was carried out behind closed doors with no wider consultation.[80] There was also considerable pressure exerted by anti-choice groups to include the unborn's right to life in the draft Northern Ireland Bill of Rights in the aftermath of the 1998 Belfast (Good Friday) Agreement.[81] This was ultimately unsuccessful, however it dominated the human rights consultation process detracting from deeper considerations of women's needs for reproductive choice.[82] To nurture this stance, Northern Irish politicians repeatedly proclaimed that the people of Northern Ireland were opposed to abortion. As Alex Easton declared in Stormont in 2007: 'A moral, and Christian, principle is embedded in the heart of the vast majority of people in Northern Ireland, who consider a child to be a precious gift from God and believe that every child has a right to life from the moment of conception in the womb'.[83] This rhetoric has continued despite

[77] The former Secretary of State for Health, Ms. Virginia Bottomley, has said that abortion is 'offensive to the overwhelming majority' of those in the North. The Northern Irish House of Commons has also been depicted as possessing only a 'pro-abortion minority'. *Hansard N.I. (Commons)*, 8 October 2013, vol. 88, no. 4, col. 42.

[78] Mr. Buchanan, 'Abortion', Private Members' Business, NI Assembly, vol. 24, 22 October 2007, http://www.niassembly.gov.uk/assembly-business/official-report/reports-07-08/22-october-2007/.

[79] Mr. O'Dowd. 'Abortion', Private Members' Business, NI Assembly, vol. 24, 22 October 2007, http://www.niassembly.gov.uk/assembly-business/official-report/reports-07-08/22-october-2007/.

[80] Rossiter, *Ireland's Hidden Diaspora*, p. 19.

[81] E. V. Fegan and R. Rabouche, 'Northern Ireland's Abortion Law', *Feminist Legal Studies*, 11:3 (October 2003), pp. 221–54, 241–42.

[82] Ibid., p. 242.

[83] Private Members' Business, 'Abortion', NI Assembly, vol. 24, 22 October 2007, http:leenan//www.niassembly.gov.uk/assembly-business/official-report/reports-07-08/22-october-2007/.

opinion polls which, since the 1990s, have indicated that a majority of the Northern Irish population favoured more widely available legal abortion services *in* the province. A 1994 Northern Irish poll found that 79% favoured abortion when a woman's health was endangered; 72% for rape and incest pregnancies and 59% for severe foetal abnormality.[84]

The political refusal to address the incongruous position of Northern Irish women seeking abortions or even to provide clear guidelines as to the legal situation in Northern Ireland led feminist and pro-choice campaigner, Rossiter, to claim that leaving the issue to Stormont 'means putting women's rights in the hands of evangelical Taliban'.[85] Indeed, there have been growing attempts by groups, particularly women's organisations, to force reform that would bring Northern Ireland in line with the rest of the UK. In the 1980s the Northern Ireland Abortion Campaign was established to raise awareness and appeal to Westminster to stop allowing Northern Ireland to evade the issue of abortion and force UK citizens to migrate and pay for abortion care. For example, it sent 600 wire coat hangers to Westminster each with a copy of a flight ticket attached and the words 'These are the two ways in which NI women get abortions'.[86] No reform was forthcoming.

As in the Republic of Ireland, this placed the onus on the courts to make decisions regarding the legality of abortions. In fact, writing in the *Northern Ireland Legal Quarterly*, Tony McGleenan argued that the reason why the law was suddenly being tested in the Northern Irish courts was precisely because of 'an increasing awareness amongst the public, and…the medical profession, of the penumbra of doubt surrounding abortion law and the unfortunate consequences of that uncertainty'. He also believed that the 'saga' of the X case in the Republic 'forced many to reflect on the state of our own law and to ponder whether Northern Ireland has its own X case waiting in the wings'.[87] Indeed, in 1993, the Belfast High Court considered the case of a fourteen-year-old ward of court who was pregnant. She did not want to continue with the

[84] C. Francome, 'Attitudes of General Practitioners in Northern Ireland Toward Abortion and Family Planning', *Family Planning Perspectives*, 29:5 (1997), p. 234.

[85] Rossiter, *Ireland's Hidden Diaspora*, p. 19.

[86] M. Hill, *Women in Ireland: A Century of Change* (Belfast: Blackstaff, 2003), p. 199. Anti-abortion reform bodies include LIFE and Precious Life.

[87] T. McGleenan, 'Bourne Again? Abortion Law in Northern Ireland After Re K and Re A', *Northern Ireland Legal Quarterly*, 45 (1994), pp. 389–94, p. 390.

pregnancy and was suicidal. The local health board wanted legal clarity on the girl's right to travel for an abortion. However, querying why the abortion could not be carried out in the province, the presiding Judge Sheil was informed by a senior consultant that no doctor was willing to perform a termination as the girl's mother opposed it and there was a 'perceived uncertainty' about the legality of such an abortion.[88] Prof. William Thompson of Queen's University, Belfast explained: 'Every time you carry out an abortion, you are left wondering if you are going to get arrested for it'.[89] The judge therefore ruled that a termination should be carried out not in Northern Ireland but in Liverpool.[90] Writing in 1994, Suzanne Breen noted that 'the status of all other abortions, including those performed during the first 28 weeks of pregnancy to save the life of the mother, remains a grey area'.[91] She claimed that the availability of abortion in Northern Ireland depended on the 'moral views and legal boldness of the doctors concerned'.[92] One might conclude that this ruling clarified that abortions in such cases as the threat of suicide were, therefore, legally permissible. Indeed, following that ruling 77 induced abortions were carried out in NI hospitals from 1997 to 1998 and 78 from 1998 to 1999, indicating that the medical profession felt more certain regarding the cases in which abortion was legal after the ruling.[93]

However, the Alliance for Choice (AfC) was formed in the late 1990s in direct response to continued legal uncertainty and because of dismay at the way abortion was surreptitiously dealt with during the 1998 peace talks. It was a broad-based, non-funded organisation of women and men from all faiths campaigning for the extension of the 1967 Abortion Act to Northern Ireland.[94] A major push for this came in 2008 when AfC tried to get a bill through Westminster that would extend the 1967 act, the fear being that when policy and justice powers were devolved to the Northern Ireland Assembly, abortion would never be legalised. As Anna Lo,

[88] Ibid. p. 392.

[89] S. Breen, 'Uncertainty of North's Abortion Laws "Could Violate Human Rights"', *Irish Times*, 14 November 1994.

[90] Brennan, 'The State of Abortion Law in Northern Ireland', pp. 251–53.

[91] Ibid.

[92] Ibid.

[93] L. Smyth, 'The Cultural Politics of Sexuality and Reproduction in Northern Ireland', *Sociology*, 40:2 (2006), p. 675.

[94] Rossiter, *Ireland's Hidden Diaspora*, p. 18.

of the Alliance Party, explained to a British audience: 'The *status quo* means that a woman in Bangor, Wales, has the right to free access to abortion on the NHS, while a woman from Bangor, Co. Down, has no access and instead has to travel to Britain and pay privately for a termination. Yet both women pay the same taxes'.[95] The male heads of all the other main parties: Peter Robinson (DUP), Gerry Adams (Sinn Féin), Sir Reg Empey (Ulster Unionists) and Mark Durkan (SDLP) signed a letter urging MPs not to support the amendment.[96] The four main Northern Irish churches also wrote asking MPs to oppose the move, citing the peace process as justification. In Derry, pro-choice activists staged a '40 women protest' to mark the number of women that they estimated left the province weekly to access abortion in Britain. Pro-choice campaigners feared a secret deal between Downing Street and the Democratic Unionists to ensure that the abortion amendment would not be dealt with due to insufficient time.[97] As predicted, Westminster did not rise to the challenge and the amendment was not passed. In the *Nursing Times*, Jane Wright courageously wrote 'not just as a nurse but as one of the thousands of women who has had to travel to England to end a pregnancy'. She called on those in Westminster and the Northern Ireland Assembly to hang their 'heads in shame', concluding: 'The truth is that the problem of abortion is at best exported and, at worst, life and health is risked by refusing women safe legal abortion'.[98]

A Softening of the Moral Lens?

The political response in Northern Ireland has been not only to block the extension of the 1967 act but also to refuse to provide clear guidance regarding when an abortion can be legally performed. This situation has resulted in women who are lawfully entitled to abortions in the

[95] Quoted in H. McDonald, '"Last Chance" to Legalise Abortions in Northern Ireland', *The Guardian*, 19 October 2008.

[96] Bloomer and O'Dowd, 'Restricted Access to Abortion in the Republic of Ireland and Northern Ireland: Exploring Abortion Tourism and Barrier to Legal Reform', pp. 366–80, p. 368.

[97] McDonald, '"Last Chance" to Legalise Abortions in Northern Ireland'.

[98] J. Wright, 'Failure to Extend the Abortion Act Puts Lives of Women in Northern Ireland at Risk', *Nursing Times*, 23 November 2008.

province being denied them.[99] This prompted demands for clearer legal guidelines for medical practitioners.[100] When the Minister for Health, Social Services and Public Safety, Michael McGimpsey, began the process of getting guidelines through the Northern Ireland assembly, he met continuous opposition from the DUP and Sinn Féin, both claiming that this was an attempt to introduce abortion. The minister had to clarify that the 'purpose of the guidance is not to make it easier or more difficult to obtain an abortion in Northern Ireland; the reason for producing the guidance is to clarify the existing law on abortion and to provide clinical and good practice guidance to health professionals'.[101] The guidelines were finally published (significantly without an official press release) in 2010. However, in 2013 these were again revised, stating: 'Health and social care professionals have a legal duty to refuse to participate in, and must report, any procedure that would not be lawful in Northern Ireland'. These guidelines have been criticised by the Royal College of Midwives and John O'Kelly, Northern Ireland chair of the Royal College of General Practitioners, claimed that they actually had made the legality of abortion more opaque: 'We probably muddled along until recent times', but the guidance 'has muddied the waters even further'.[102] The fact that these guidelines have still not been ratified indicates the level of official ambivalence.[103] In consequence, healthcare professionals have noted: 'It is hardly surprising that many [medical professionals] avoid all conversation of the subject of abortion…preferring to remain silent, as they cannot be accused of breaching NI law'.[104]

[99] R. J. Cook, 'Transparency in the Delivery of Lawful Abortion Services', *Canadian Medical Association Journal*, 180:3 (2009), pp. 272–73, p. 272.

[100] Smyth, 'The Cultural Politics', pp. 665, 671–75. Northern Ireland is one of 24 countries, including New Zealand, where mental health is a ground for legal abortion. Singh, Remez, Sedgh, Kwok and Onda, *Abortion Worldwide 2017: Uneven Progress and Unequal Access*, p. 115.

[101] 'Abortion', Private Members' Business, NI Assembly, vol. 24, 22 October 2007, http://www.niassembly.gov.uk/assembly-business/official-report/reports-07-08/22-october-2007/.

[102] C. Dyer, 'Abortion Numbers Halve in Northern Ireland as Doctors Fear Prison', *British Medical Journal*, 352:1 (8 January 2016), p. 135.

[103] For a sense of the multiple attempts and failures to supply guidelines see, 'Abortion Practice and Provision in Northern Ireland—Factsheet—FPA' (8 October 2014), https://www.fpa.org.uk/sites/default/files/northern-ireland-abortion.pdf.

[104] P. Daniels, P. Campbell, and A. Clinton, 'The Current State of Abortion Law and Practice in Northern Ireland', *British Journal of Nursing*, 22:6 (2013), pp. 36–38.

Table 5.1 Department of Health and Social Services and Public Safety, Northern Ireland abortion and termination of pregnancy figures, 2006–2012[a]

	Medical abortion	*Termination of pregnancy*
2006–2007	76	57
2008–2009	71	44
2010–2011	73	43
2011–2012	56	35

[a]Table extracted from Bloomer and O'Dowd, 'Restricted Access to Abortion in the Republic of Ireland and Northern Ireland,' p. 371

In this atmosphere of ambiguity, the rate of legal abortions being performed within Northern Ireland has continued to fall: in 2014–2015, for example, 16 terminations were recorded in hospitals in Northern Ireland, a decline of 7 procedures from the previous year and a significant decline from the 43 procedures recorded in 2010–2011 (see Table 5.1).[105]

In October 2012, the issue of abortion rights was cast centre stage by the opening of Northern Ireland's first private abortion clinic in Belfast. The centre's programme director, Dawn Purvis bravely declared the opening of this Marie Stopes clinic to be 'great news for the people of Northern Ireland', because now their 'family planning and sexual health needs' could be met in a way not previously possible in Northern Ireland.[106] Indeed, while the centre offered a range of services relating to contraception and sexual health, the focus of attention was almost entirely on its abortion service. Although the clinic was constrained by the law it offered women a medically-safe environment, on Irish soil, to avail of the abortion pill or a medical abortion. The reaction from anti-abortion groups comprising Catholics, members of the Free Presbyterian Church and other groups, was swift and bullish: they united across denominational lines to close the clinic down and to attempt to change the minds of women who sought to enter the clinic. One of the main anti-abortion groups, Precious Life, declared itself 'outraged' at

[105]While the impact of the abortion pill must be considered in these declining rates, so too must the impact of fear and uncertainty about the medical profession's decision-making.

[106]Cited in H. McDonald, 'Northern Ireland's First Private Abortion Clinic to Open in Belfast', *The Guardian*, 11 October 2012.

the clinic's opening, warning: 'There will be an outcry from the people, from government and from the churches'.[107] This reaction might have appeared perplexing to any onlooker: the Marie Stopes clinic could only facilitate abortions that were legal under Northern Ireland's strict laws. As Purvis explained, that meant that abortions would only be carried out in the clinic when there was a serious threat to the physical or mental health of the mother.[108] The opposition therefore stemmed from a desire to prevent *any*, even legal, abortions happening on Irish soil.

Ironically, it was not the protests that closed the clinic's doors in 2017, but the British government's move to fund abortions for women from Northern Ireland in England. This reform was initiated outside the Northern Ireland Assembly by the Westminster Labour MP Stella Creasy and it means that Northern Irish women now qualify for NHS care and thus no longer have to find the resources for a private procedure costing in the range of £500–2000.[109] In principle, the fact that Northern Irish women were recognised as taxpayers who should not be required to pay the NHS twice for a service, was a good one, but this was also an evasive manoeuvre as it avoided the central problem: these abortions should be a right that Northern Irish women could avail of *in* Northern Ireland.[110] Yet again, the British government showed no appetite to take on the Northern Irish political establishment in defence of a right granted to all other female British citizens. As Purvis noted, on the day of the clinic's closure: 'We continue to export the problem and it's really only a local solution that will help women the way they should be helped in terms of this healthcare service you can access anywhere else in the United Kingdom except in Belfast'.[111]

[107] Ibid.

[108] Purvis outlined this in an interview of RTÉ Radio *Today with Pat Kenny* show. See, 'Marie Stopes to Provide Abortions at New Private Clinic in Belfast', *RTÉ News*, 11 October 2012, https://www.rte.ie/news/2012/1011/341154-marie-stopes-abortion-belfast/, accessed 26 October 2018.

[109] 'Northern Irish Women Win Access to Free Abortions as May Averts Rebellion', *The Guardian*, 29 June 2017, https://www.theguardian.com/world/2017/jun/29/rebel-tories-could-back-northern-ireland-abortion-amendment.

[110] A. Ferguson, 'Closure of Marie Stopes Belfast Clinic Ends Five Years of Hostility', *Irish Times*, 8 December 2017.

[111] Ibid.

With the closure, the *Irish Times* declared the end of 'five years of hostility'.[112] It was true that the clinic encountered almost continuous enmity from anti-abortion protesters, but it had also been tenaciously supported by many others and had assisted thousands of women during its lifetime. It was transformative in changing the landscape of the abortion debate in Northern Ireland. The protests outside the building revealed the ugly and less than compassionate side to elements of the anti-abortion campaign,[113] while the numbers of women willing to face those protesters to enter the clinic highlighted the need for its services. Although it was lamented that the clinic had not been able to assist couples facing an Fatal Foetal Anomaly [hereafter FFA] diagnosis, its very existence provided a 'supportive public space', in which women could start to tell their abortion stories.[114]

Conclusion

Several factors contributed to the campaign to ensure that abortion was not legalised on the island of Ireland, but central to this was the agency of Irish women travelling in significant numbers for abortions outside of their respective states which eased the pressure on legislators to introduce reform.[115] In Northern Ireland, the main political parties sought to outdo each other in their anti-abortion posturing while day after day women boarded boats and planes to seek the health care they were denied at home. In the Republic the government sought, on more than one occasion, to subvert the X case ruling that would have allowed abortion for mental health reasons. In both states there was minimal official consideration of how abortion migration might impact, negatively or otherwise, on women and their health. Instead, 'a strange kind of morality... governed by geography', pertained on the island.[116]

[112] Ibid.

[113] Women were offered escorts to help them pass the protesters and fend off any attempts to intimidate the women entering the Marie Stopes clinic. For descriptions of some of these protests see, H. McDonald, 'Anti-abortion Activists Protest at Belfast Clinic Opening', *The Guardian*, 18 October 2012.

[114] This point was made in conversation with Dawn Purvis.

[115] Maguire, 'The Changing Face of Catholic Ireland', pp. 335–58; McAvoy, 'From Anti-Amendment Campaigns to Demanding Reproductive Justice', p. 17.

[116] D. Walsh, 'Plebiscites Cannot Stop Sad Procession to England', *Irish Times*, 29 November 1997.

CHAPTER 6

Abortion in Exile, 1967–2018

Abstract Irish women travelling for abortion hailed from all corners of Ireland, from Belfast to Bandon, from Armagh to Waterford: the border was of little consequences to the reality of the Irish abortion experience. Any woman resident on the island of Ireland who wished or needed to assert their 'reproductive autonomy' and terminate a pregnancy for any reason other than her imminent death in the Republic of Ireland and long-term and permanent risk to her health in Northern Ireland had to leave the island. This chapter explores the impact of the secrecy, silence and shame that dominated Irish abortion history on the women at the centre of the experience. In both states abortion implicitly became a woman's problem; one she must resolve outside the state. There was little discussion or engagement with what abortion travel meant in health, psychological or real terms for the thousands of people impacted. This chapter highlights how it was women themselves that finally forced a reframing of the Irish abortion journey, by speaking out and breaking the silence.

Keywords Abortion in exile · Reproductive autonomy · Travel · Britain · Fatal Foetal Anomaly · Rape · Inequality · Trauma · Abortion stories

Irish women travelling for abortion hailed from all corners of Ireland: the border was of little consequences to the reality of the Irish abortion

L. Earner-Byrne and D. Urquhart, *The Irish Abortion Journey, 1920–2018*, Genders and Sexualities in History,
https://doi.org/10.1007/978-3-030-03855-7_6

experience. Any woman resident on the island of Ireland who wished or needed to assert their 'reproductive autonomy' and terminate a pregnancy for any reason other than her imminent death in the Republic of Ireland and long-term and permanent risk to her health in Northern Ireland had to leave the island.[1] Secrecy, silence and shame dominated the Irish abortion experience: women forced to travel to access abortion services were isolated from the many other Irish women who were, for decades, literally in the same boat. One woman recalled her shock when she realised, many years after her own abortion, how many other women had the same experience: 'What astonished me is the number of women who have stories to tell you back. I'm talking about my generation and our experiences with unwanted pregnancies. It is clear a path was beaten to London all through the 1960s and early 1970s'.[2] Even as the numbers of women travelling increased throughout the 1980s and 1990s, it often remained a solitary affair in which women, sometimes accompanied by male partners, parents or friends, but often alone, relied on the kindness of strangers to provide them with information, accommodation and, at times, with funds and emotional support. Until recently, there was little political engagement with the reality of the Irish abortion ban which covers pregnancy as a result of rape or incest, repeated caesareans, exposure to rubella and radioactive material, organ failure and diabetes, difficult previous pregnancies, allergies to contraception, psychological issues, multiple miscarriages, still births and cases of Fatal Foetal Anomaly [hereafter FFA].[3] In both states abortion implicitly became a woman's problem; one they must resolve outside the state. There was little discussion or engagement with what abortion travel meant in health, psychological or real terms for the thousands of people impacted: the women seeking abortions, their partners and families, and the medical professionals involved in Ireland and in Britain. It was, however, women who had abortions who finally forced a reframing of the Irish abortion journey,

[1] Mullally, 'Abortion Law: Rights Discourse, Dissent and Reproductive Autonomy', p. 213.

[2] '"Stories of Abortion": By People Who Have Been Through It', *Irish Times*, 25 March 2012.

[3] E. Porter, 'Culture, Community and Responsibilities: Abortion in Ireland', *Sociology*, 30:2 (1996), pp. 279–98, p. 289.

Table 6.1 Department of Health figures for abortion in England and Wales with Northern Ireland and Republic of Ireland residency declared, 2002–2012[a]

	NI	*ROI*
2002	1391	6522
2004	1280	6217
2006	1295	5042
2008	1173	4600
2010	1101	4402
2012	905	3982

[a]Table extracted from Bloomer and O'Dowd, 'Restricted Access to Abortion in the Republic of Ireland and Northern Ireland: Exploring Abortion Tourism and Barrier to Legal Reform', pp. 366–80, p. 372

by speaking out and breaking the silence. This chapter tells some of their stories.[4]

The Women Behind the Statistics

The number of women travelling for abortions from both Northern Ireland and the Republic of Ireland augmented steadily until the early 2000s; in 1990 4064 Irish women had abortions in Britain[5]; in 2001 the figure was 6673. As one woman observed in 2000: 'If the numbers were what counted, we would surely be viewed as normal as the girl next door'.[6] However, in 2012 the collective figures for Irish women travelling for abortion were under 5000 for the first time in decades (68% from the Republic of Ireland and 15% from Northern Ireland) and this was the eleventh consecutive year in which the figure fell (see Table 6.1).[7] More common use of the abortion pill, although illegal, explains much of this decline.

[4]The oral testimony material is collated from books, newspapers and online sources and social media.

[5]This was an increase of 343 on the previous year. Eileen Quinn, St. Saviour's Priory, Dublin to Editor 'Abortion', *Fermanagh Herald*, 4 January 1992.

[6]'Marie's Story', in M. Ruane, *The Irish Journey: Women's Stories of Abortion* (Dublin: Irish Family Planning Association, 2000), p. 13.

[7] *Belfast News-Letter*, 12 July 2013.

In 2000, in her ground-breaking book, *The Irish Journey: Women's Stories of Abortion*, Medb Ruane observed: 'Irish society needs women's silence to keep its good opinion of itself'.[8] Ruane's work sought to give a voice to the women behind the Irish abortion story and, published by the Irish Family Planning Association [hereafter IFPA], it represented an important contribution to a long process of making public the reality of the Irish abortion journey. As Ruane noted:

> Yet under the white-washed surface, people's sisters, mothers, wives and girlfriends; along with neighbours, teachers, waitresses, poets, students, lawyers, homemakers, doctors, farmers, media workers, factory workers, artists, information technologists, civil servants, bank officials and more, are taking long, sad, journeys to keep official Ireland squeaky clean.[9]

However, the atmosphere in which these women came forward to tell their stories for Ruane and the IFPA's project was still one of 'fear and recrimination' meaning that the contributors' anonymity had to be preserved through assumed names.[10] There had been a consistent attempt in the media coverage—driven by female journalists—to insist that Irish women who 'travelled to Liverpool' and beyond were not 'abnormal', rather they were 'nice girls' fearful of their families' reaction.[11] As the women's affairs correspondent, Mary Cummins, highlighted in 1993: 'THE majority of Irish women who go to Britain for abortions do not come from the margins of society but are part of its mainstream with a high proportion of them attending church regularly'.[12] These characterisations of women who had abortions as church-goers were clearly attempts to work against the pervasive stigmatisation of these women. As 'Carol', one of the women who told her story to Ruane, recalled after

[8] Ruane, *The Irish Journey*, p. 6.

[9] Ibid.

[10] This was noted by Noeleen Hartigan, Chairperson of the IFPA in Ruane, *The Irish Journey*, p. 57.

[11] M. Maher, 'Counselling and Guilt and Ignorance', *Irish Times*, 20 February 1981. Female journalists also played a significant role in promoting birth control as a women's issue in the early 1970s and raising the social and economic issues relating to abortion. See, A. Stopper, *Mondays at Gaj's: The Story of the Irish Women's Liberation Movement* (Dublin: Liffey Press, 2006), p. 173.

[12] Mary Cummins, Women's Affairs, 'Most Women in Abortion Study Are Churchgoers', *Irish Times*, 12 August 1991.

her abortion in *c.* 1978: 'Many times through the years I have had to listen to people give out about abortion. Saying things like "What sort of a woman could kill her own child? They should go to prison, it's murder." "Those women are sluts." I just sit there and say nothing'.[13]

In fact, as the Director of Pregnancy Counselling at the IFPA, Sherie de Burgh explained: 'Not every woman will have an abortion, but any woman could have one'.[14] One thing that distinguished these women was the ability to raise the money to travel, but apart from this, all other evidence suggests Irish women who seek abortions are a diverse group. Indeed, the issue of money and the ability to pay is a recurring theme in all the coverage of the Irish abortion story. During the 1970s it took an average of five to eight days from the first counselling session to final discharge and cost £70.13—the equivalent of £1060 today.[15] As a Dublin-based counsellor who referred women to abortion clinics in Liverpool explained in the 1970s: 'The Liverpool clinic…have told us about Irish girls who get straight off the boat and ask the nearest policemen where they can get an abortion. It's horrific. Money is often a problem but the women always get it together if they have to pawn, beg, borrow or steal'.[16] In 1994, 'Beth', a single mother of a six-year-old, became pregnant after rape. She could not tell anyone or seek help getting the money together to travel, 'I couldn't borrow from family or friends because they would want to know what it was for. So I took out a loan'. 'Beth' was still repaying this loan two years later.[17]

There was a general realisation that poor women 'overburdened with children and unable to pay for an abortion', would have little choice but to endure repeated pregnancies.[18] Indeed, 'Anna', a mother with two

[13] Ruane, *The Irish Journey*, p. 21.

[14] Ibid., p. 5.

[15] The cost of an abortion is now estimated at £400–2000. C. Dyer, 'Abortion Numbers Halve in Northern Ireland as Doctors Fear Prison', *British Medical Journal*, 352:1 (8 January 2016), p. 135.

[16] 'These Women Are Not Selfish', *Irish Times*, 10 July 1978.

[17] K. Malik, 'It's the One Thing That Unites Us', *Independent on Sunday*, 13 November 1994 reproduced by Kenan Malik on his website Pandaemonium on 4 February 2015, https://kenanmalik.com/2015/02/04/united-against-abortion/, accessed 20 August 2018.

[18] Anne Figgis, Templeogue, Dublin 12 to Editor. 'The Abortion Referendum', *Irish Times*, 7 July 1983.

children, recalled considering selling her body to raise the money for her abortion:

> I had no money…I rang a person I vaguely knew, and knowing that they had paid someone handsomely for sex, I approached them with the first choice being a loan, and if not, I would do "the other". I was so desperate. And felt so bad that I had sunk so low as to even contemplate this.

In the end 'Anna' was given a loan.[19] As recently as 2010, Mary Muldowney confirmed that the same social inequalities remain inherent in the Irish *status quo* regarding abortion; she cites a woman who 'borrowed money from a loan shark in order to go to Britain to have an abortion and then she came back and she got beaten black and blue because she couldn't afford to pay'.[20] In 2018, a young woman posted about her abortion five years previously, when she had been sixteen, painting a vivid picture of the stress of having to travel and pay for her procedure:

> I skipped school so that I could work extra days in my part time job in order to make ends meet and lied to my family and forged fake letters to my school; I couldn't sleep with worry in case of any additional costs as I could not have sustained this. Would I be refused treatment if I was £40 short? What would I do then?[21]

This young woman's testimony reveals the strategies some had to employ in order to arrange, pay for and keep secret an abortion. This was a young woman, forced to miss school and lie about her whereabouts, and her worry about being financially unable to pay for an abortion remained with her years afterwards.

[19] 'Anna's Story' in Ruane, *The Irish Journey*, p. 40.

[20] M. Muldowney, 'Breaking the Silence: Pro-choice Activism in Ireland Since 1983', in J. Redmond, S. Tiernan, S. McAvoy, and M. McAuliffe (eds), *Sexual Politics in Modern Ireland* (Dublin: Irish Academic Press, 2015), pp. 127–50, p. 142.

[21] Anonymous posted at 1.08 p.m. 20 August 2018 on the Facebook page 'In Her Shoes—Women of the Eighth', https://www.facebook.com/InHerIrishShoes/posts/226856324655459:0?__tn__=K-R.

Travel as Trauma

In 2000 Sherie de Burgh insightfully summarised the impact of adding travel to the abortion experience:

> Carrying a sense of shame for your country is a terrible burden. Ireland's refusal to accept the reality of abortion, and acknowledge the humanity and rights of the individual woman behind the statistics, bestows a sense of shame on women and creates secrecy and isolation to reinforce that feeling.[22]

The personal cost for individual women of the 'shame' surrounding abortion in Ireland has been reinforced by secrecy, fear and the need to travel. De Burgh notes that women's stories highlighted 'the negative effect of having to travel'.[23] While the fact that Irish abortion has been an experience carried out in secret is widely acknowledged, the impact of exile on the women forced to travel is rarely explored. If you have to travel to end an unwanted, unviable or dangerous pregnancy, what impact does it have on you, your decision-making or your emotional and physical health? As one woman recalled of her experience: 'For all the talk of women travelling to England for abortions, I'd never thought of the actual journey. The travelling somehow compounds everything. Before that it was all mostly a private crisis, now it became public with cover stories and lies'.[24]

Many Irish women who experienced abortion travel expressed a sense of rejection. In 1994, 'Amy' from a 'small Protestant community in County Antrim' needed an abortion and did not know where to turn. She was eventually helped by the NIFPA and a sympathetic doctor to arrange an abortion in London, but 'the trip was traumatic' as she had never been more than 20 miles from home before and 'the strain of lying and the terror of being found out was overwhelming'.[25] In 2000, one married woman said she 'felt a bit like the poor relation, creeping

[22] Sherie de Burgh, Preface to Ruane, *The Irish Journey*, p. 4.

[23] Ibid., p. 5.

[24] 'Kate's Story' in Ruane, *The Irish Journey*, p. 55.

[25] Malik, 'It's the One Thing That Unites Us', *Independent on Sunday*, 13 November 1994.

in the back door. I can see where the sense of shame comes from'.[26] While, in 2012, another married woman articulated her 'fury' at 'being forced into a corner by those who know little or nothing about how a young pregnant girl feels'. She believed she had been silenced and damaged by having to travel for her abortion: 'I deeply resent those, my husband included, who demand my silence, and I wish people realised how "going to England" damages one's sense of worth'.[27] Others 'felt quite angry about the legislation in Ireland', which 'forces women to travel abroad' as though they were 'morally deficient people in a pure-white state'.[28] In a post on *In Her Shoes—Women of the Eighth*, a woman from Northern Ireland recalled how having to travel for an abortion in Manchester in 2014 made her feel 'like a criminal'. In particular, her post underscored how the necessity to travel had added to the emotional *and* physical trauma involved: 'The whole thing was awful, I was in so much pain after but I had nowhere to go, we sat in a café for a few hours and then headed back to the airport'.[29] For this woman, being in a strange place, away from home or somewhere safe to go, exacerbated the physical and mental pain involved in her abortion process.

While for some women the fact that there were other Irish women present at the abortion clinic was a comfort, for others there was no sense of solidarity due to the overriding feelings of fear and shame. As 'Jean' remembered: 'I knew about the numbers of women who travel, but I also felt like the only one in the world'.[30] She was a mother of seven and believed she could not cope with an eighth pregnancy; the practical issues were 'enormous'; she had to travel alone because the alternative was to 'invent a weekend away. That would involve endless lies to the children, family and friends. Going alone was by far the better option in one way, but it felt lonely and frightening to travel alone for an operation'. Apart from the emotional damage and the burden of shame, travelling for an abortion also presents a myriad of logistical problems

[26]'Jean's Story' in Ruane, *The Irish Journey*, p. 45.

[27]'"Stories of Abortion": By People Who Have Been Through It'.

[28]Ibid.

[29]'Single mum' posted 1.40 p.m., 26 August 2018 on the Facebook page 'In Her Shoes—Women of the Eighth', https://www.facebook.com/InHerIrishShoes/posts/230994587574966:0?__tn__=K-R.

[30]'Jean's Story' in Ruane, *The Irish Journey*, p. 44.

and for many the practical arrangements and the lies that must be told come to dominate the decision-making process.

This was equally an issue in Northern Ireland where women who did not qualify under the very strict rules for abortion had to travel to Britain and pay for an abortion just as their southern counterparts had to do. As already noted, it is only since 2017 that Northern Irish women qualify for NHS care and thus no longer have to find the resources to pay for an NHS abortion.[31] However, this policy change has been described by Mara Clarke of the Abortion Support Network as 'a plaster to the disease that is the abortion law in Northern Ireland…there will always be cases of people who cannot travel, or for whom travel to another country is a hardship'.[32] Ann Rossiter's pioneering study *Ireland's Hidden Diaspora*, published in 2009, did much to raise awareness regarding the particular situation of Northern Irish women. Rossiter notes that they often felt like a 'suspect race' when they had to travel for abortions during the Northern Irish conflict.[33] She explains that the Northern Irish abortion trail was 'also a story of Loyalists unwittingly caught in the fault lines of empire and war, of nationalists and the ethnic stereotyping… there is the incongruity of having to pursue a termination available to her British compatriots across the water, but not on her own turf'.[34] Indeed, many Northern Irish women posted stories on social media during the recent 2018 abortion referendum campaign highlighting the similarities between their abortion experiences and those of women from the Republic.

In reality the abortion journey is both stressful and expensive and the need to travel makes the abortion process harder for all women, but in particular for those in the lowest socio-economic bracket.[35] Abortion activists, journalists and healthcare professionals highlighted this particular inequality since the 1970s, but it had no real impact on policymakers

[31] 'Northern Irish Women Win Access to Free Abortions as May Averts Rebellion', *The Guardian*, 29 June 2017, https://www.theguardian.com/world/2017/jun/29/rebel-tories-could-back-northern-ireland-abortion-amendment.

[32] Mara Clarke, director of the Abortion Support Network (ASN), *Belfast Telegraph*, 31 August 2017.

[33] Rossiter, *Ireland's Hidden Diaspora*, pp. 34, 135.

[34] Ibid., p. 34.

[35] Daniels, et al., 'The Current State of Abortion Law and Practice in Northern Ireland', p. 362.

in either state. Rural women too have longer and more expensive journeys and are often leaving more conservative communities in which secrecy is even more of a priority. Women, already marginalised in Irish society, find that abortion travel presents the greatest barrier to accessing abortion services, hence, in recent years women seeking asylum in Ireland have featured in some of the most tragic cases. A stark reminder of this came in early May 2018 when the London coroner's report on the 2012 death of Aisha Chithira was released. Malawi-born, but resident in Ireland from 2009, Chithira had a 'significant gynaecological history'. Her need for a visa to access abortion services in London delayed travel for approximately a month and, close to 20 weeks gestation, some clinics would not accept her. After the procedure in London, she collapsed in a taxi and later died as a result of intra-abdominal bleeding.[36] As Carl O'Brien reported: 'She died on her own—in a strange taxi, in a foreign city, on a street she didn't know'. Placing her death in the wider context of Ireland's abortion regime, he stated: 'it raises wider issues around the real experiences of women who seek abortions following crisis pregnancies. The hardship is often compounded by poverty, language difficulties, travel restrictions for migrant and asylum-seeking women'.[37] Her death made front-page news but, like those who sadly preceded her, did not lead to immediate reform.[38] There are groups doing much to raise awareness of the particular challenges for migrants and ethnic minorities in Ireland, for example, Migrants and Ethnic-minorities for Reproductive Justice, which highlights how adversely affected migrants are by the necessity to travel for abortion services.[39]

Unsurprisingly the trauma of travelling for an abortion surfaces repeatedly in Irish abortion narratives; in fact, it is often central to their telling. Indeed, as research by Ann Rossiter and Mary Sexton revealed, the main point of difference that sets Irish women apart from other

[36] 'Death of Woman to Travelled to UK for Abortion "Deeply Sad"', *RTÉ News*, 1 May 2018, https://www.rte.ie/news/uk/2018/0501/959477-inquest/, accessed 5 September 2018.

[37] C. O'Brien, 'Troubling Insight into Lonely World of a Crisis Pregnancy', *Irish Times*, 23 July 2013.

[38] *Belfast News-Letter*, 23 July 2013, front page.

[39] Facebook page 'Migrants and Ethnic-Minorities for Reproductive Justice—MERJ', https://www.facebook.com/pg/MERJIreland/about/?ref=page_internal, accessed 30 August 2018. See the later consideration of the Ms Y case in 2014.

women who have had abortions is the fact that they must travel: the journey defines the experience, compounds the sense of exile and makes the social rejection real.[40]

Disrupted Health Care

Implicit in the necessity of leaving one's state for an abortion is disrupted health care: a woman must leave her own healthcare system. This involves a host of health risks and complications. The problems start at the most basic level, with women unaware of their legal position and consequently fearful to ask direct questions or reveal medical information. For example, many women believe that they are breaking the law by travelling to procure an abortion outside Ireland, although it is perfectly legal. 'Miriam', who had an abortion in 1995, noted that in a subsequent pregnancy she was too fearful to tell her doctor of her termination: 'When I went for antenatal visits I didn't know whether to tell them I'd had an abortion or not. I had a friend and she had told the hospital, and they had written TOP [termination of pregnancy] in large letters on her chart'. Indicative of the fact that this kind of fear was widespread, her doctor also advised her to adopt a coded approach to informing the hospital: 'I went back to my GP and he advised me just to look at the doctor and say I'd had a miscarriage and she might know, or cop on'.[41] This is a common dilemma for Irish women, fearful of the reaction to previous abortions or unsure what the legal situation is; they conceal their health history. 'Miriam's' story also indicates that the medical profession often share these fears with their patients.

Travelling also leads to delays, meaning the timing of a procedure is often not dictated by considerations of a woman's health and gestation period, but rather is driven by the cost of surgical and non-surgical procedures, familial and work responsibilities and, in more recent years, the availability of cheap flights. Waiting for a passport or a visa can cause similar delays.[42] The result is that Irish women are more likely to have terminations after ten weeks gestation than their English or Welsh

[40] A. Rossiter and M. Sexton (ed.), *The Other Irish Journey: A Survey Update of Northern Irish Women Attending British Abortion Clinics*, 2000/2001 (London: Marie Stopes International, 2002).

[41] 'Miriam's Story' in Ruane, *The Irish Journey*, pp. 26–27.

[42] See the above discussion of the fatal 2012 case of Aisha Chithira.

counterparts.[43] Later gestation also augments the cost of the procedure and the risk of medical complications. One young woman, who posted her story on social media in August 2018, noted that she was seven weeks pregnant when she travelled to Manchester for an abortion, but she still opted for a surgical procedure rather than having to wait for a second pill.[44] In other words, this woman opted for a more high risk and invasive procedure, because she could not afford more time in a place far from home. Her need to travel for an abortion directly impacted on her decision regarding which medical option to choose. In other cases women arrive with virtually no medical knowledge about their pregnancy and this can mean there are undiagnosed health conditions such as high blood pressure or low iron. These conditions can result in the procedure not being performed on their first visit forcing them to travel for a second time. These are the often-hidden consequence of a regime that forces women by default to travel to access abortion care in another state.

An untold number of women have had to deal with pain or other complications following travelling for an abortion and have been too scared to seek help upon their return. In 2017, Caoimhe Anglin recalled how she had bled heavily for weeks after her abortion carried out in England and was in 'agony', but was too fearful to seek help at an Irish hospital. She explained how difficult the journey home had been: 'you're so tired and then you have to get on a train, go to the airport and then wait on the floor of Manchester airport in Terminal 3, which has no seats while you're doubled-over in pain'.[45] This happens as there are no guidelines for managing the associated trauma or medical complications such as haemorrhage, which may occur on the return journey.

[43] Bloomer and O'Dowd, 'Restricted Access to Abortion in the Republic of Ireland and Northern Ireland', p. 372; R. Fletcher, '"The Pro-Life" Absolutes, Feminist Challenges: The Fundamentalist Narrative of Irish Abortion Law 1986–1992', *Osgoode Hall Law Journal*, 36:1 (1998), pp. 1–62, p. 9.

[44] Anonymous post at 1.08 p.m. 20 August 2018 on the Facebook page 'In Her Shoes—Women of the Eighth', https://www.facebook.com/InHerIrishShoes/posts/226856324655459:0?__tn__=K-R.

[45] Claire Scott, 'Irish Woman Who Was Left "Bleeding Heavily" After Abortion Was Afraid of Going to an Irish Doctor', *DublinLive.ie*. 8 November 2017, https://www.dublinlive.ie/news/dublin-news/irish-woman-who-left-bleeding-13871041, accessed 2 September 2018. Caoimhe Anglin created an art exhibition of stories from women who have been affected by the 8th amendment.

Healthcare workers in the Republic and in Northern Ireland also emphasise that women are fearful of disclosing when they have taken the abortion pill. This fear stems for the fact that it is illegal in both states in Ireland to take abortion pills and could result in a prison sentence.[46] While no woman has been prosecuted for taking abortion pills in the Republic and abortion law is due to be changed in 2019, in 2016 a woman was prosecuted in Northern Ireland under the 1861 Offences Against the Person Act for inducing her own abortion and received a two-month suspended sentence.[47] More recently a mother who helped her fifteen-year-old daughter import abortion pills after she had become pregnant is also potentially facing trial.[48]

One of the common themes throughout the history of abortion on the island of Ireland has been confusion over how to interpret the law. It is little wonder that lay people are confused regarding their rights, when the medical profession appears equally uncertain. This fear of the law, which is sometimes misplaced, coupled with the continued stigma of abortion means that some practitioners in Ireland refuse to even discuss abortion with a woman. Other women have been denied an abortion even when their medical consultant is supportive. In December 2010, Wexford woman, Michelle Harte told her story of having to travel for an abortion in Britain despite being diagnosed with cancer. She had originally been euphoric to discover her pregnancy, but her oncologist advised it was 'too big a risk' to her health. Although, the hospital's ethics forum had to first authorise the abortion, her doctors 'felt

[46]Women in the Republic of Ireland can face a prison sentence not exceeding 14 years under the Protection of Life During Pregnancy Act, 2013 until the law is changed.

[47] *Belfast Telegraph*, 7 April 2016.

[48]A. Erwin, 'Mother Facing Belfast Trial for Allegedly Procuring Teen Daughter's Abortion Wins Permission to Challenge Prosecution', *Belfast Telegraph*, 16 January 2017. The mother is seeking a judicial review of the decision to prosecute her in the criminal court. On 20 September 2018 the North's Chief Justice adjourned the case to allow the prosecutors to make a formal submission to the High Court in Belfast on the human rights implications of the case in the wake of the recent Supreme Court ruling. In June 2018 the Supreme Court rejected an appeal over the legality of Northern Ireland's restrictive law. It should be noted that the majority of judges said the law was 'incompatible with human rights in cases of fatal foetal abnormality and sexual crime. See, 'Case of Woman Accused of Obtaining Abortion Pills for Daughter Adjourned', *Irish Times*, 20 September 2018.

there wouldn't be a problem'.[49] However, almost two weeks later she was informed that the ethics committee of Cork University Hospital had advised that it did not consider her life to be in 'immediate threat', hence she was not eligible for a termination in Ireland.[50] She was thus obliged to travel outside the state for a termination in order to continue her cancer treatment. However, her abortion was further delayed by the need to get an up-to-date passport and make arrangements with a hospital in Britain for her termination. During her short pregnancy she had not received cancer treatment and her condition had deteriorated significantly. She was so ill that she required help to board the plane. Michelle had been living on disability benefit since her cancer diagnosis and thus she needed a loan to fund her abortion and was unable to afford even a taxi from the airport.

The week before Michelle told her story, the European Court of Human Rights [ECHR] ruled against Ireland in the *A, B* and *C* cases[51]; the court found that Ireland had 'failed to give full effect to the constitutional right of allowing abortion in Ireland where the life of the mother is at risk'.[52] The Irish government had argued that Ms C could have accessed a legal abortion in Ireland, if she had established, in line with the X case, 'as a matter of probability, that there was a real and substantial risk to [her] life ...and that this risk could only be averted by the termination of her pregnancy'.[53] The ECHR rejected this argument and it was clear that Michelle Harte's right to a legal abortion *in* Ireland on the basis of the X case had also not been vindicated.[54] In November 2012, the Irish state settled with Michelle Harte, but posthumously as by this time she had died of her cancer.[55] The *Irish Times* asked: 'Did the

[49] C. O'Brien, 'Why Is Simple Treatment Not Available Even When a Mother's Life Is at Risk?', *Irish Times*, 21 December 2010.

[50] Cork University Hospital was at pains to clarify that the ethics forum merely 'guided, but not instructed' staff in relation to such issues. C. O'Brien, 'Hospital Says Ethics Body Did Not Instruct Staff', *Irish Times*, 22 December 2010.

[51] C. O'Brien, 'Lawful-Abortion Process Shrouded in Uncertainty', *Irish Times*, 22 December 2010.

[52] F. Lambe, 'Abortion Nightmare for Cancer Sufferer Michelle', *Irish Independent*, 28 December 2010; C. O'Brien, 'Why Is Simple Treatment Not Available Even When a Mother's Life Is at Risk?', *Irish Times*, 21 December 2010.

[53] Editorial, *Irish Times*, 22 December 2010.

[54] Ibid.

[55] P. Cullen, 'State Settled with Cancer Patient', *Irish Times*, 22 November 2012.

decision not to allow her a legal abortion, and the ensuing delay, cause her immediate death? Clearly, not. Has it shortened her life? Almost certainly'.[56] In 2018, in the context of an abortion campaign focused on women's health, her doctors came forward confirming that in their professional opinion she 'might still be alive were it not for the Eighth Amendment'. Professor Louise Kenny recalled:

> I found myself dealing with a woman with complex medical conditions and I had to say to her that not only can I not treat you here in Ireland, and you have to travel abroad, but I cannot even pick up the phone on your behalf and refer you – It goes against everything I've been trained to do as a doctor'[.][57]

Many of the details of Michelle Harte's case underscored the injustices of the abortion situation in Ireland. The fact that she had to travel delayed her abortion meaning she could no longer have a medical abortion, but required a surgical intervention. Her doctor could not legally refer her, so she had to communicate her complex medical history to doctors in England. She had to borrow to afford the procedure and, despite medical advice, left hospital early because she could not afford to miss her Ryanair flight home. Once in Ireland, she recalled: 'I was very much left on my own. There was no follow-up or support, either medically or emotionally'. Her motivation for speaking out was to prevent other women suffering as she had, but her question hung over Ireland for another eight years: 'why is it that such a simple medical treatment is not available, even when a mother's life is at risk?'[58]

Many people were also unaware until recently that abortion is not a legal option for couples who receive a diagnosis of FFA. In such cases some people decide to terminate the pregnancy for complex and personal reasons, but once they make this decision they too are on their own. The care needs of these women are distinct, but until recently this did not feature prominently in Irish abortion discourse. In Northern Ireland Sarah Ewart publicised her experience of abortion travel in 2013 to seek

[56] Editorial, *Irish Times*, 22 December 2010.

[57] *Irish Times*, 13 May 2018. The headline read 'Mother might still be alive but for Eighth Amendment'.

[58] O'Brien, 'Why Is Simple Treatment Not Available Even When a Mother's Life Is at Risk?'

a reform in the law for cases such as hers. After receiving an FFA diagnosis at 19 weeks, she highlighted her stark reversal of views: 'Before this happened to me, I didn't agree with abortion but this is medical – this is a dead body that I am being forced to carry in Northern Ireland'.[59] As a result of her case, David Ford, the Northern Ireland Minister of Justice, was pressed on a timeline for amending the law in cases of FFA, but his reply emphasised the complexity of both criminalising and reforming abortion provision in the province: as a criminal law the department of justice would consider it, but the production of guidelines lay, as in the Republic of Ireland, within the department of health's remit. However, noting the 'very difficult and emotional circumstances of lethal foetal abnormality', Edwin Poots, the Minister of Health, implicitly sought to distinguish these cases from other 'morally suspect' abortions: 'I believe that all the couples want to have the child in the first place. They are not people who want to engage in some form of dispensing with a pregnancy because it was unplanned'.[60] He clearly wished to paint these parents as different from the 'types' of people who seek abortions in other circumstances. In this way, he and many others seek to keep a moral firewall between abortion in the case of FFA and abortion in 'crisis pregnancies'.

Organisations such as Termination for Medical Reasons [hereafter TMR] have done much to raise awareness about the difficulties faced by Irish couples who receive an FFA diagnosis. TMR's Chairwoman, Dr. Siobhán Donohue explained that the group believed the eighth amendment was preventing couples with an FFA diagnosis from receiving proper medical care in Ireland. Couples who do not wish to continue with a pregnancy after such a diagnosis in Ireland are forced to leave their Irish medical care team and travel outside the state and face repatriating their infant's remains alone. For example, in 2018 'Ciara' was told her baby had three sets of chromosomes meaning it was incompatible with life. Apart from the tragedy of this pregnancy, it also posed a physical risk to 'Ciara' and medical guidelines indicated that such pregnancies should be terminated. 'Ciara's' doctors refused on the basis of Irish law. 'Ciara' and her husband travelled to Liverpool on Valentine's day for a termination. Afterwards, she recalled her horror when a nurse asked:

[59] 'Woman's Abortion "Ordeal" Considered by NI Health Officials', *BBC News*, Northern Ireland, 9 October 2013, https://www.bbc.co.uk/news/uk-northern-ireland-24458241, accessed 5 September 2018.

[60] *Hansard N.I. (Commons)*, 3 December 2013, vol. 90, no. 2, p. 31.

'You've got a ten-hour journey home again, so how are you going to keep your baby cold?' 'Ciara' recounted carrying her baby's white coffin on her knees in the car, packing it with cold packs each hour to keep his remains cool. Even in her grief she was most hurt by the implicit evidence that others had preceded her in this particular Irish funeral procession: 'you come out at the port in Dublin and you get stopped by Customs and there's guards there, and the saddest thing was that we pulled up to the guard, and he looked in and he just waved us on, as if he'd seen it a million times'.[61] Indeed, in 2016, Dr. Caroline Gannon, one of only two paediatric pathologists in Northern Ireland, resigned after having to advise a couple to bring foetal remains home in a cooler bag.[62]

Many couples like 'Ciara' and her husband have recently come forward and described the devastation of receiving an FFA diagnosis. Not all choose to end the pregnancy, but those who do find that having to travel adds an intolerable strain to an already very difficult situation. The indignity of then having to smuggle one's baby's remains back into the country was repeated in countless stories over the course of the 2018 abortion referendum. Similarly, in Northern Ireland this issue has prompted calls for reform: in 2018 a report from a working group drawn from the departments of health and justice in Northern Ireland recommended that the law should be changed to provide for abortions in such cases.[63] In this report health professionals argued that 'retaining existing legal constraints would continue to place an unacceptable burden on women's health and wellbeing'.[64] Crucially, the report declared that the:

[61] Aisling Kenny, 'Eighth Amendment—Women's Stories', *RTÉ News*, https://www.rte.ie/news/ireland/2018/0508/961047-eighth-amendment-womens-stories/, accessed 30 August 2018.

[62] *Belfast Telegraph*, 15 September 2016. The headline read: 'Call for change to abortion law after doctor quits over foetus is cooler bag'.

[63] 'Healthcare and the Law on Termination of Pregnancy for Fatal Foetal Abnormality: Publication of Report (25 April 2018)', https://www.health-ni.gov.uk/news/health-care-and-law-termination-pregnancy-fatal-fetal-abnormality-publication-report-0, accessed 2 September 2018. See, Department of Justice and Department of Health, *Report of the Working Group on Fatal Fetal Abnormality: Healthcare and the Law on Termination of Pregnancy for Fatal Fetal Abnormality* (11 October 2016).

[64] *Report of the Working Group on Fatal Fetal Abnormality*, p. 5.

> most compelling cases for change was the overall recognition by those health professionals who spoke to the group that the existing legal framework prevents them from fully meeting their duty of care to all women in this situation and therefore denies those women who wish to terminate the pregnancy, access to proper standards of health care.[65]

Conclusion

The consequences of abortion in exile are manifold: fear of prosecution for both patient and practitioner; the health risks of abortion travel; the lack of bereavement counselling and moving from one healthcare system to another all raise challenges for the patient–carer relationship and for the provision of aftercare. Given this, it is quite remarkable that some continue to claim that the ban on abortion has not damaged the health of mothers or endangered their lives. Those like Sarah Ewart, organisations such as TMR, publications like Ruane's (along with the IFPA) and Rossiter's and the individual women who have spoken out are all part of a growing narrative to bravely make public the reality of abortion travel in order to encourage reform. As Ewart observed, 'I do have a sense that things are changing. Before people wouldn't even have talked about it. Me speaking out has made the public understand that there are more reasons why you might need an abortion'.[66] This discourse has been transformative.

[65] Ibid.

[66] 'I Needed an Abortion but My Consultant Told Me: "I'm Not Going to Prison"', *Guardian*, 7 January 2016, www.theguardian.com/world/2016/jan/07/northern-ireland-abortion-ban-sarah-ewart-interview, accessed 5 September 2018.

CHAPTER 7

Trusting Women, 2000–2018

Abstract To date, in practical terms a woman in Dublin and Belfast will have had a very similar experience when seeking an abortion: she will more than likely have had to travel out of her state. However, since the 1980s there has been one crucial difference between the two states, which feeds directly into the fact that it is the Republic of Ireland that will change its abortion laws first. Since 1983 the Republic of Ireland has been constantly 'talking abortion'; it has experienced six abortion-related referendums each involving debate and protest. By comparison, in Northern Ireland there has been little pretext for debating the jurisdiction's abortion laws. This chapter explores how the momentum for reform in the Republic culminated in the overwhelming mandate to repeal of the eighth amendment in May 2018. It also reveals how this situation has increased the focus on Northern Ireland, which is now virtually alone in Western Europe in clinging to its restrictive abortion regime.

Keywords Reproductive health · Reform · Maternal death · Abortion pills · Suicide · Repeal · Savita

Thus far the histories of both of the states on the island of Ireland have been examined to highlight similarities, differences and the ways in which the states have played off each other in relation to women's

L. Earner-Byrne and D. Urquhart, *The Irish Abortion Journey, 1920–2018*, Genders and Sexualities in History,
https://doi.org/10.1007/978-3-030-03855-7_7

reproductive health and sexuality. However, since the 1980s there has been one crucial difference between the two states, which feeds directly into the fact that it is the Republic of Ireland that will change its abortion laws first. Thus the country originally cast as the more conservative of the two has travelled fastest down the by no means inevitable road of reform. Since 1983 the Republic of Ireland has been constantly 'talking abortion'; it has experienced six abortion-related referendums each involving debate and protest. By comparison, in Northern Ireland there has been little pretext for debating the jurisdiction's abortion laws. As we have argued, abortion debates have been transformative in the Republic of Ireland. This is evident not only in terms of moving the abortion debate beyond abstract morality to lived experience but also in bolstering many pro-choice campaigners' belief that change is possible in the North.

1983 as Pandora's Box

In many respects the pro-life groups that lobbied for an amendment to the Irish constitution to prevent the legalisation of abortion in the early 1980s ensured that the country would debate a subject, which had been previously largely ignored, for the next four decades. During the 1983 referendum campaign all the risks of such an unequivocal ban were outlined: the fact that it would not prevent abortion but export it; the inequitably of forcing women to travel; the dangers to women's health; the possibility that even women in danger would be denied an abortion due to fear of prosecution; the fate of survivors of rape, incest and domestic violence and the danger of dealing with an issue as complex as abortion in a constitution. As history demonstrates, those warnings were prescient. The wording of the eighth amendment to the constitution proved difficult to interpret and created a sufficient 'chill' factor which meant that medics were, on occasion, afraid to provide legal abortions even when a woman's life was in danger. Members of the medical and legal professions began warning of the potential risks in this regard as soon as the amendment passed, just as liberals and feminists began a decades-long campaign to 're-orient the nation's ostensible "pro-life" ethos towards a concern for the lives and health of girls and women, rather than foetal life exclusively'.[1] This was to be a long, painful and vocal process of debate, which sought constantly to weigh up the rights of 'unborn children' and pregnant women.

Since 1983 the eighth amendment has often been interpreted in a particularly negative way; as Jennifer Schweppe observed, it was '*prohibiting* the dissemination of "abortion information" and *preventing* a young girl travelling to England'.[2] Ruth Fletcher further argued that the Irish courts gave 'legal authority to a fundamentalist view of the value of foetal life', when it denied Irish citizens their rights under European Community Law to information regarding abortion services legally available outside the Irish state.[3] Fiona de Londras and Mairéad Enright have also demonstrated how '[R]ather than recognize the 8th Amendment as protecting life in all its richness and depth, successive courts and governments have been content to assume that it only protects the bare condition of being alive'. In effect, once a woman becomes pregnant in Ireland her 'constitutional rights are subordinated to the right to life of the unborn and circumscribed by the constitutional status of "mother"'.[4] A graphic illustration of this is that while the Health Service Executive's (HSE) National Consent Policy notes that usually adults are allowed to refuse medical treatment, pregnant women's rights are limited as 'there is significant legal uncertainty regarding the pregnant woman's right to refuse/treatment in circumstances in which refusal would place the life of a viable foetus at serious risk. In such circumstances, legal advice should be sought as to whether an application to the High Court is necessary'.[5] Hence not only can Irish women be denied medical treatment because of the rights of the unborn child, they are also occasionally

[1] L. Smyth, 'The Cultural Politics of Sexuality and Reproduction in Northern Ireland', *Sociology*, 40:4 (2006), pp. 663–80, p. 673; Connolly, *The Irish Women's Movement*, pp. 155–86; Muldowney, 'Breaking the Silence: Pro-choice Activism in Ireland Since 1983', pp. 127–50.

[2] Schweppe, 'Introduction', in Schweppe (ed.), *The Unborn Child, Article 40.3.3 and Abortion in Ireland*, pp. 1–14, p. 11.

[3] Fletcher, '"The Pro-life" Absolutes, Feminist Challenges: The Fundamentalist Narrative of Irish Abortion Law 1986–1992', pp. 1–62, p. 6.

[4] F. de Londras and M. Enright, *Repealing the 8th: Reforming Irish Abortion Law* (Bristol: Policy Press, 2018), p. 2.

[5] Cited in de Londras and Enright, *Repealing the 8th*, p. 9.

forced to undergo medical procedures against their will for the same reason.[6]

Feminist journalists, women's groups, students and civil liberty groups and various bodies of professionals and scholars from all disciplines have almost continuously been making the case for reform by highlighting the cost to women of the eighth amendment. This constant conversation grew louder throughout the 1990s as various cases proved the human cost of Ireland's abortion regime. The Republic also embarked on a journey of self-reflection prompted by revelations of clerical child abuse and the treatment of unmarried women and their children, compounded by a profound economic crash in 2008.[7] Many of the revelations regarding clerical abuse were driven by witness testimony and the stories told by these survivors had a powerful impact on Irish society, not least because they provided a model of how to speak 'truth to power'.[8] In the 2000s many of those affected by abortion and the law in Ireland began to break the silence with their personal testimony. Indeed, Laury Oaks argues, there has been a shift in public discourse to acknowledge that abortion is now an accepted part of the Irish experience.[9] In 2008 the Safe and Legal in Ireland campaign developed three short videos in a series entitled *Stop the Silence, End the Stigma*; it was ranked the second most watched posting on YouTube in Ireland.[10]

[6] Ibid., p. 10.

[7] For a discussion of the impact of these events see, L. Earner-Byrne, 'Child Sexual Abuse, History and the Pursuit of Blame in Modern Ireland', in K. Holmes and S. Ward (eds), *Exhuming Passions: Memory and the Pressures of the Past in Australia and Ireland* (Dublin: Irish Academic Press, 2011), pp. 51–70.

[8] See, for example, *Report of the Commission to Inquire into Child Abuse* [known as the Ryan Report] (1999).

[9] L. Oaks, '"Abortion Is Part of the Irish Experience, It Is Part of What We Are": The Transformation of Public Discourse on Irish Abortion Policy', *Women's Studies International Forum*, 25:3 (2002), 315–33, p. 315.

[10] McAvoy, 'From Anti-amendment Campaigns to Demanding Reproductive Justice', pp. 15–47. See, http://www.youtube.com/profile_videos?user=SafeAndLegalIreland&p=d.

Savita

The death of Savita Halapanavar in Galway in October 2012 further transformed the Irish abortion debate in a country that was in the midst of change.[11] Savita Halapanavar was seventeen weeks pregnant when she presented at University Hospital Galway with back pain; she died of septicaemia in the hospital a week later. The HSE report into her death noted that doctors had refused the patient and her husband's request for a termination 'due to their assessment of the legal context in which their clinical professional judgement was to be exercised': the HSE then quoted the eighth amendment.[12] The report further noted that the medical approach had been one of 'await events' and 'to monitor the foetal heart in case an accelerated delivery might be possible once the foetal heart stopped'.[13] Doctors waited until they were sure Savita's life was in danger—they waited too long.[14] The European Court of Human Rights had already ruled in 2010 that Ireland had not provided clarity on the legal availability of abortion in circumstances where the mother's life was at risk and this cost Savita her life.

In October 2017, the Committee on the Eighth Amendment to the Irish Constitution[15] heard 'if it weren't for the Eighth Amendment, Savita Halappanavar would be alive today'.[16] Indeed, in a discourse emerging since Savita's death, the legal position in relation to abortion was reframed as 'immoral' with even some practising Catholics arguing

[11] A. O'Conor, 'How the Death of Savita Halappanavar Changed the Abortion Debate', *Irish Examiner*, 28 October 2017; H. McGee, 'How the Yes and No Sides Won and Lost the Abortion Referendum', *Irish Times*, 26 May 2018.

[12] Health Services Executive [HSE], *Final Report: Investigation of Incident 50278 from Time of Patient's Self Referral to Hospital on 21st of October 2012 to the Patient's Death on 28th October 2012* (June 2013), p. 5.

[13] Ibid.

[14] The story first broke in the *Irish Times* on the 14 November 2012 ('Woman "Denied a Termination" Dies in Hospital', *Irish Times*, 14 November 2012).

[15] The committee was established in April 2017 to consider the Citizen's Assembly report in relation to the Eighth Amendment of the Constitution. See, https://www.oireachtas.ie/en/committees/32/eighth-amendment-constitution/.

[16] 'Risks to Health, 'Including Physical Health, of Pregnant Women: Professor Sabaratnam Arulkumaran, Dr. Peter Boylan and Dr. Meabh Ní Bhuinneáin'. Joint Committee on the Eighth Amendment of the Constitution Debate, 18 October 2017, https://www.oireachtas.ie/en/debates/debate/joint_committee_on_the_eighth_amendment_of_the_constitution/2017-10-18/3/, accessed 2 August 2018.

that: 'The majority of Catholics trust women to grapple with tough moral questions about when and whether to continue a pregnancy, and to make those decisions for themselves'.[17] In this narrative the eighth amendment is seen as having established 'false equivalencies' between the life of the unborn and the pregnant woman.[18] Yet, not all were willing to embrace this: head of the Catholic Church in Ireland, Cardinal Seán Brady, reiterated the church's opposition to abortion in the aftermath of Savita's death.[19] However, there was a huge national and international reaction to her death and the government was finally forced to legislate for the X case of 1992 and honour the electorate's vote in the referendums of 1992 and 2002 (Fig. 7.1).[20]

In 2013 the Irish government introduced the Protection of Life During Pregnancy Act [PLDPA], which maintained the criminality of abortion in all cases with the exception of risk to the mother's life, making clear that this included the risk of suicide. It also provides for imprisonment of up to fourteen years for those found guilty of performing an abortion or procuring one, including the consumption of abortion pills. However, from the outset this legislation proved problematic. In 2014, the case of Miss Y poignantly exposed its shortcomings: Miss Y had sought an abortion after seeking asylum in the Republic and discovering she was pregnant as a result of rape.[21] Despite repeatedly claiming she was suicidal at the prospect of carrying the pregnancy to full term, she was not given the care she needed as a result of a series of delays. When she was finally assessed by a three-doctor panel under the provision of the 2013 act, it confirmed she was suicidal but concluded her pregnancy was too far progressed for termination. Finally, after a hunger strike and forcible rehydration by order of the Irish courts, her baby was delivered by caesarean section at 25 weeks gestation. The infant was placed in the care of the state.

[17] J. O'Brien, 'Catholics Have Evolved in Their Thinking About Abortion', *Irish Times*, 16 January 2018. Jon O'Brien is president of Catholics for Choice, based in Washington, DC.

[18] O'Brien, 'Catholics Have Evolved in Their Thinking About Abortion'.

[19] 'Cardinal Brady Reiterates Opposition to Abortion in Christmas Message', *Ulster Herald*, 27 December 2012.

[20] *Report of the Joint Committee on the Eighth Amendment of the Constitution* (December 2017), p. 35.

[21] K. Holland, 'Timeline of Ms Y Case', *Irish Times*, 4 October 2014.

Fig. 7.1 Protest to government buildings following the death of Savita Halappanavar, Dublin, 17 November 2012. Photo by Derek Speirs

Evidence relating to the 2013 act given to the Joint Committee on the Eighth Amendment to the Constitution claimed 'an under-resourced psychiatric service for pregnant women' meant that 'psychiatrists with minimal experience of dealing with women in pregnancy could be required to assess cases'.[22] Prof. Veronica O'Keane, a senior lecturer in the Department of Psychiatry at Trinity College Dublin, also argued that the process of accessing an abortion was so complex that the procedure was not guaranteed even in cases where a woman or girl was eligible. As she emphasised, the women expected to navigate this complex legislation were vulnerable women at risk of suicide.[23] De Londras and Enright have further highlighted that the legislation makes 'no reference to the pregnant woman's wishes or voice' and '[o]nce she has sought abortion

[22] *Report of the Joint Committee on the Eighth Amendment of the Constitution* (December 2017), p. 8.

[23] K. Holland, 'Accessing Abortion Is a "Lottery" Under Irish Rules', *Irish Times*, 12 June 2017.

Table 7.1 Abortions in the Republic of Ireland, 2014–2016[a]

	Illness	*Emergency*	*Suicide*
2014	14	9	3
2015	14	9	3
2016	8	16	1

[a]'Ireland Through the Years', *RTÉ News*, 24 April 2018, https://www.rte.ie/news/ireland/2018/956963-abortion-timeline/, accessed 2 September 2018

care, all other decisions are made by someone else: by medics, by lawyers, by courts, by "the system"'.[24] Any woman that can travel or find another option, for example, the abortion pill, will do so rather than go through PLDPA process. Thus, as Marguerite McCarthy, a crisis pregnancy counsellor with One Family, noted, it is usually the most economically and socially disadvantaged women in Ireland who rely on this legislation.[25] The Dáil recorded that *c.* 30 legal abortions were carried out within the jurisdiction in 2013[26] and later figures suggest that the application of these amended grounds remains limited (Table 7.1).

Repealing the Past

In January 2018, the Republic of Ireland's Minister for Health, Simon Harris, announced a referendum on whether or not to repeal the eighth amendment. He rooted his decision in Irish history *and* in Irish geography: he itemised the number of women that had left each county and emphasised that they were 'real women' who drew their historical lineage back to Ann Lovett:

> I think of another cold January like this one in 1984 when the 15 year-old Ann Lovett gave birth alone to her son beneath a statue of Our Lady. The

[24]de Londras and Enright, *Repealing the 8th: Reforming Irish Abortion Law*, p. 8.

[25]A point made by Marguerite McCarthy during a discussion with Kathy Sheridan on the *Irish Times'* The Women's Podcast 'Ordinary Women and the 8th Referendum', 14 May 2018, https://soundcloud.com/irishtimes-women/ep-216-ordinary-women-and-the-8th-referendum, accessed 2 June 2018.

[26]Bloomer and K. O'Dowd, 'Restricted Access to Abortion in the Republic of Ireland and Northern Ireland: Exploring Abortion Tourism and Barrier to Legal Reform', pp. 366–80, p. 371.

Fig. 7.2 Rise and Repeal march and rally, Dublin, 24 September 2016. Photo by Derek Speirs

> death of Ann and her baby son in these stark and lonely circumstances is a memory that chills us still and one we should not forget. We now arrive at another moment on a long journey, starting with the insertion of the eighth amendment of the Constitution in 1983[27]

Echoing the words of women's groups in the previous decades, he stressed that these women were 'our friends, neighbours, sisters, cousins, mothers, aunts and wives'. He also framed this referendum in the *zeitgeist* of a Republic in the process of deciding 'what kind of a country we want to be and what kind of a society we are'.[28] In May 2015 Ireland had become the first country to legalise same-sex marriage through popular vote and it was in the spirit of this 'new Republic' that many

[27] Minister for Health, Simon Harris, 'Report of the Joint Committee on the Eighth Amendment of the Constitution: Statements', *Dáil Eireann Debate*, 17 January 2018, https://www.oireachtas.ie/en/debates/debate/dail/2018-01-17/25/, accessed 2 September 2018.

[28] Ibid.

perceived this abortion campaign. Following the success of that referendum, the 'Rise and Repeal campaign' was inaugurated to campaign for a referendum to repeal the eighth amendment. This was a cross-party organisation of those in favour of repeal and it organised annual repeal marches, short YouTube videos and strike days to highlight the issue (Fig. 7.2).[29] It was in this climate that the government accepted the report of the Oireachtas Joint Committee on the Eighth Amendment of the Constitution and outlined that if the people voted to repeal the eighth amendment, it would legislate for abortion up to twelve weeks' gestation.[30] The fact that Irish women could and were importing the abortion pill was a decisive factor in this regard.

Those who were vehemently opposed to repealing the amendment resurrected the 'floodgate' trope that accompanied the majority of Irish liberal-based reforms from divorce to contraception. As retired judge to the High Court, Bryan McMahon, wrote to the *Irish Times*, 'this is only the beginning of a journey to an even more liberal abortion regime in future'.[31] Anti-abortion groups such as the 'Pro-Life campaign',[32] 'LoveBoth'[33] and the Iona Institute[34] argued that the eighth amendment had saved lives and had not endangered women's lives. In essence, these organisations claimed that repeal would lead to 'abortion-on-demand', a phrase coined to imply that abortion would become a casual option for

[29]For further details see, Abortion Rights Campaign website https://www.abortionrightscampaign.ie/tag/rise-and-repeal/; See, for example, Rise and Repeal, 2016 video https://www.youtube.com/watch?v=j0OaAz7N07k and https://www.youtube.com/watch?v=P7JYEfXi2RM.

[30]The Oireachtas Joint Committee on the Eighth Amendment of the Constitution made this recommendation following extensive consultation with various groups in December 2017. See, for example, 'Oireachtas Committee to Recommend Unrestricted Abortions up to 12 weeks', *Irish Times*, 12 December 2017.

[31]Letter to the Editor, *Irish Times*, 4 May 2018.

[32]The Pro-Life Campaign Described Itself as a 'Non-denominational Human Rights Organisation and Drew Its Members from the Original Pro Life Amendment Campaign Group of 1981', https://prolifecampaign.ie/main/about/, accessed 2 September 2018.

[33]'For Anyone Who Thinks "Abortion Is Happening Anyway"', https://loveboth.ie/the-eighth-amendment-saves-lives-i-am-a-prove/; 'This Referendum Is Not About Maternal Health'—Letter to Boylan and Mahony. https://loveboth.ie/referendum-is-not-about-maternal-health/, accessed 2 September 2018.

[34]S. MacDonald, 'Proposed Abortion Law Is in No Way Restrictive: Iona Institute', *CatholicIreland*.net, https://www.catholicireland.net/proposed-abortion-law-no-way-restrictive-iona-institute/, accessed 2 September 2018.

women and a ghost of the 1970s argument that birth control would lead to promiscuity.

Pro-repeal groups conjoined under the banner 'Together for Yes', describing themselves as a 'national civil society campaign to remove the 8th Amendment'.[35] While established political commentators were initially critical of what they perceived to be a lack of momentum in the 'Yes' campaign, this was partially because they failed to understand it as a grassroots feminist movement.[36] As Miriam Lord would later claim, this campaign was 35 years in the making and it was built on the backs of every Irish woman or couple exiled: 'Woman by woman, story by story, year upon year, day after day. The rocks and pebbles of countless unjust ordeals and small tragedies piled up after each furtive trip to Liverpool and beyond'.[37] The Yes campaign's crowd-funding initiative, begun in April 2018, gave the first concrete indication of public support: it raised €322,000 by the end of its first day.[38] Shying away from aggressive campaigning, the Yes campaign prioritised conversations—a model adopted during the same-sex marriage referendum. One of these initiatives was #HearMeOut, which urged people to: 'Put the kettle on, start a conversation, send a letter, an email or even a text asking a person in your life to hear you out'.[39] The Together for Yes campaign emphasised three 'Cs': Compassion, Care and Change. It was initially hard to assess the country's mood with broadcasting rules insisting on a 'balance' in debate (which effectively demands equal

[35] Co-Directors were Grainne Griffin (founding member of Abortion Rights Campaign), Orla O'Connor (Director of the National Women's Council of Ireland) and Ailbhe Smyth (veteran feminist campaigner and former head of Women's Studies at UCD), https://www.togetherforyes.ie/about-us/our-executive/, accessed 31 August 2018. The National Women's Council of Ireland had been issuing policy papers in relation to abortion for some time and did much work to create an environment amenable to a second referendum on the eighth.

[36] See, for example, the episode of *Today with Sean O'Rourke* RTÉ 1, 26 May 2018.

[37] M. Lord, 'It Took 35 Years to Build This Stunning Result', *Irish Times*, 28 May 2018.

[38] A. Connelly, 'Eighth Amendment: A Look Back at the Campaigns', *RTÉ News*, https://www.rte.ie/news/analysis-and-comment/2018/0528/966631-eighth-amendment-campaign-ends/, accessed 31 August 2018.

[39] I. Hamilton, 'Campaign Getting Irish People Have Real Convos About Abortion Away from Internet Disinformation', *Mashable*, 21 May 2018. See, https://mashable.com/2018/05/21/hearmeout-campaign-irish-referendum/?europe=true#6m6JVx-BRasql, accessed 20 September 2018.

airtime for all points of view) in radio and television debates (although this does not apply to social media) and with polls notoriously unreliable, people remained unsure throughout the campaign. The use of personal stories, however, united both campaigns. While figureheads of each side spoke on radio and television, it was the individual stories, for and against abortion that dominated.[40] Ultimately it was compassion for those experiencing the trauma of abortion travel at first hand which prevailed: 'There is a momentum and a power behind the Yes side in the upcoming referendum that I don't think we've seen before in this country. Women and girls the length and breadth of our little island are standing up to say they won't be shamed and punished for their biology any longer'.[41]

The referendum to repeal the eighth amendment to the Irish constitution was held on 25 May 2018. That evening the exit polls began to hint at an extraordinary event—the Irish people had voted to trust women by a two-thirds majority.[42] Not only this, but the polls revealed no gender or rural–urban divide and that the main reason people had voted for abortion reform was because of a belief in women's right to choose.[43] The next day the streets were full of women in tears. This was personal. The weight of history was lifting for so many people who had not known they were burdened by it and who had not considered themselves politicised. As feminist journalist and campaigner Susan McKay declared: 'So this is what liberation feels like. I am crying. I am laughing. I am so, so proud'.[44] When the official result was read a huge crowd

[40] See, for example, 'Abortion and Me: Share Your Story', *Irish Times*, 4 May 2018.

[41] Lydia Walsh, Cork: Letter to the Editor, *Irish Times*, 4 May 2018.

[42] On the evening of 25 May both the *Irish Times* and the national broadcaster RTÉ released exit polls indicating a significant majority for repeal: 68 and 69.4% respectively. 'Landslide: Two Exit Polls Predict Ireland Has Voted Overwhelmingly to Repeal the Eighth Amendment', *Journal*, i.e. http://www.thejournal.ie/referendum-yes-no-4035145-May2018/, accessed 2 September 2018.

[43] The RTÉ poll showed that 62% of those who voted did so to support the woman's right to choose, 55% said that they thought risks to the health or life of a woman was an important factor, while 40% said pregnancy as a result of rape or incest was a reason. This poll also showed that 72.1% of women and 65.9% of men voted to repeal. RTÉ poll conducted by Behaviour and Attitudes. See, https://static.rasset.ie/documents/news/2018/05/rte-exit-poll-final-11pm.pdf.

[44] S. McKay, 'Grieving Couples Will No Longer Have to Smuggle the Remains of a Cremated Baby Back to Ireland', *Guardian*, 27 May 2018. Lord's article provides a very

Fig. 7.3 Savita Halappanavar mural, Dublin, 28 May 2018. Photo by Derek Speirs

that had packed into the square of Dublin Castle chanted one word: 'Savita! Savita!' As one Australian journalist wrote in an analysis of the result: 'if ever there was a reminder that the campaign against women's bodily autonomy is a campaign of violence, it would be the death of Savita Halappanavar.'[45] The impact of Savita's death was clear: a mural to her was created by the graffiti artist Aches beside the Bernard Shaw pub in Portobellow in Dublin on the week of the May 2018 referendum (Fig. 7.3).[46] In the days after the result hundreds of people stuck post-it

good history of the campaign and the women central to it. Lord, 'It Took 35 Years to Build This Stunning Result'.

45 Van Badham, 'Savita!': Why the Irish Abortion Vote Touched Women the World Over', *Guardian*, 30 May 2018.

46 'Savita Mural Artist: "I've Been Painting a Long Time, I've Never Seen a Reaction Like That Before', *The Journal*, i.e. https://www.thejournal.ie/savita-mural-artist-4044389-May2018/, accessed 22 October 2018.

notes on the mural giving their reasons for voting yes. One read 'came home in our droves for you', another echoed the sentiments of so many who voted to repeal the eighth amendment, 'Sorry we were too late but we are here now. We didn't forget you', and yet another, 'I voted for you Savita. May you rest in peace. You'll never be forgotten along with all the other women who have suffered. All my love'.[47] Many also laid flowers under her picture and many others were moved to tears. These notes were subsequently removed to prevent damage, photographed for posterity and sent to Savita's parents in south west India.[48]

In the wake of the referendum many campaigners, some true veterans since 1983, sought to ensure the analysis of the result reflected its feminist roots. Una Mullally, who had done so much to raise awareness among a younger generation,[49] warned of post-election analysis that wrote women's role out of the campaign: 'any analysis that does not place at its centre feminist, women-led movement is bereft'.[50] For so many feminists, the vote represented the defeat 'of those who hate us, fear us and wanted to keep us down…The nightmare is over':

> It has been a huge victory for humanity, for compassion, for empathy. We did not want any more children forced to bear children. Any more grieving couples having to smuggle remains of their cremated baby back to Ireland. Any more women allowed to die because they were pregnant and doctors were too afraid to treat them. On a south Dublin wall, a mural of Savita Halappanavar's beautiful lost face has candles around it now.[51]

Those who interpreted the scenes in Dublin castle as celebrations of abortion missed the point. An editorial of the *Irish Times* summed the

[47] K. Holland, 'Flowers, Notes and Messages Placed at Mural of Savita in Dublin', *Irish Times*, 26 May 2018.

[48] S. Burns, 'Savita Mural on Its Way to "Permanent" Location', *Irish Times*, 31 May 2018; L. Lynott, 'Mural of Savita Halappanavar Moved to New Home as Notes Left in Her Memory Sent to Her Parents', *Independent*, i.e. https://www.independent.ie/irish-news/abortion-referendum/mural-of-savita-halappanavar-moved-to-new-home-as-notes-left-in-her-memory-sent-to-her-parents-36966463.html, accessed 22 October 2018.

[49] U. Mullally (ed.), *Repeal the 8th* (London: Unbound, 2018).

[50] U. Mullally, 'Young Women Already Being Written Out of the Story of Repeal', *Irish Times*, 1 June 2018.

[51] McKay, 'Grieving Couples Will No Longer Have to Smuggle the Remains of a Cremated Baby Back to Ireland'.

mood up: 'This belongs to the women of Ireland'.[52] It was women the ban had most deeply affected, it was mainly women who had helped other women since the 1970s to secure legal and safe abortion outside Ireland, and it was also largely women who had campaigned tirelessly for that right to be available at home. However, the referendum threw the spotlight on the situation in Northern Ireland and BBC news posed the question that many now asked: 'After Ireland says Yes to abortion, what next for Northern Ireland?'[53]

Northern Irish Women as Collateral Damage

Until very recently, as Newton Emerson noted, opposition to terminations has been identified as a 'rare point of cross-community agreement', in Northern Ireland's tense political terrain.[54] Although there was always more dissent than this might suggest, in 1994, Joe Hendron of Northern Ireland's nationalist political party, the Social Democratic and Labour Party [hereafter SDLP] declared: 'We might have been fighting and killing ourselves for years but we are united when it comes to opposing abortion'.[55] However, the changing situation in the Republic has disintegrated this alliance. The SDLP, Sinn Féin, the main republican party, the liberal and centrist Alliance Party, and the Green Party in Northern Ireland now seek abortion reform. Highlighting the particular proclivities of Northern Irish politics, Emerson suggested that while Arlene Foster, leader of the main unionist party, the DUP and First Minister of Northern Ireland, appeared to have changed her mind at some stage over the last twenty-six years on abortion, the SDLP had done so in a week, and Sinn Féin had a messy conversion since 2015. In 1992, Foster, as an eager member of the Ulster Unionist Party's youth wing, castigated

[52] 'Editorial', *Irish Times*, 27 May 2018.

[53] Kelly-Leigh Cooper, 'After Ireland Says Yes to Abortion, What Next for Northern Ireland?', *BBC News*, 29 May 2018, https://www.bbc.com/news/uk-northern-ireland-44271876, accessed 2 September 2018.

[54] N. Emerson, 'Nationalists Perform Sharp U-turn on Abortion', *Irish Times*, 31 May 2018.

[55] K. Malik 'It's the One Thing That Unites Us', *Independent on Sunday*, 13 November 1994 reproduced by Kenan Malik on his website Pandaemonium on 4 February 2015, https://kenanmalik.com/2015/02/04/united-against-abortion/, accessed 20 August 2018.

the Republic's constitution as 'riddled with Roman Catholic social and political doctrine … A few examples include the Republic's stand on divorce and abortion'.[56] However, she has since become a staunch abortion critic. Sinn Féin moved to supporting abortion in cases of rape and FFA in 2015, and although it backed the repeal of the eighth amendment in the Republic, it was against the proposed legislation for abortion up to twelve weeks. However, the party voted to support abortion reform in Northern Ireland in June 2018 along lines similar to those being proposed in the Republic.[57]

In the wake of the referendum result, Michelle O'Neill, Sinn Fein's Vice-President and Deputy First Minister of Northern Ireland, implied that some unionists might be tempted by the prospect of a united Ireland because of access to abortion.[58] Arlene Foster displayed similar thinking, when she claimed that people from the Republic and nationalists and republicans in Northern Ireland, had been in touch 'not quite believing what is going on and saying they will be voting for the DUP because they believe we are the only party that supports the unborn'.[59] In a neat analogy, which summed up the entanglement of reproductive justice and political conflict on this island, Emerson claimed:

> The likelihood of unionists voting "Yes" to a united Ireland due to repeal of the Eighth Amendment is exactly the same as the likelihood of O'Neill voting "No" to a united Ireland due to the passing of the Eighth Amendment, or even less so, given that from a unionist perspective this is all happening in a foreign country.[60]

All of this says less about abortion and much more about the myopic nature of Northern Irish politics. As the Professor of Law at the

[56] Emerson, 'Nationalists Perform Sharp U-turn on Abortion'.

[57] J. McCormack, 'Sinn Féin Change Abortion Policy', *BBC News*, 18 June 2018, https://www.bbc.com/news/uk-northern-ireland-44507054, accessed 3 September 2018.

[58] M. McHugh, 'Sinn Féin Calling for Referendum on "United Ireland" Following Abortion', *Independent*, i.e. 27 May 2018, https://www.independent.ie/irish-news/politics/sinn-fin-calling-for-referendum-on-united-ireland-following-abortion-vote-36951126.html, accessed 2 September 2018.

[59] 'DUP Leader Claims Sinn Féin Voters Will Back Her Party Due to Abortion Stance', *Independent*, 28 August 2018.

[60] N. Emerson, 'Nationalists Perform Sharp U-turn on Abortion', *Irish Times*, 31 May 2018.

Fig. 7.4 7th Annual March for Choice of Abortion Rights Campaign, Dublin, 29 September 2018. Photo by Derek Speirs

University of Birmingham, Fiona de Londras, informed *The Atlantic*: 'In many ways, abortion rights in Northern Ireland has frequently been bargained away in Westminster for the support of Northern Irish parties'.[61]

What is certain is that the 2018 referendum in the Republic of Ireland has thrown abortion provision in Northern Ireland into sharp relief. On the same day as the referendum result, calls, accompanied by public protests, were made for abortion law reform in Northern Ireland (Fig. 7.4). With the Northern Ireland Assembly suspended since early 2017, claims by the DUP that abortion must remain a devolved issue are being seriously challenged. The focus is shifting to an external jurisdiction—Westminster. In July 2018 a cross-party letter, initiated by Labour MP Stella Creasy, who in 2017 led the campaign to allow Northern Irish women to have abortions funded by the NHS, from 173 politicians in both Ireland

[61] Y. Serhan, 'Ireland Repealed Its Abortion Ban: Is Northern Ireland Next?', *The Atlantic*, 29 May 2018, https://www.theatlantic.com/international/archive/2018/05/northern-ireland-abortion-ban/561383/, accessed 28 August 2018.

and the UK called on the British and Irish governments to reform Northern Ireland's abortion law:

> This is the first and critical step to ending the treatment of British and Irish women as second-class citizens, who do not enjoy the same access to healthcare as their counterparts do across these islands...ensure that the spirit of the Good Friday Agreement is upheld and the human rights of women living in Northern Ireland are respected.[62]

Moreover, with the DUP bolstering the conservative government, as Creasy highlighted, 'we don't want the women of Northern Ireland to be the collateral damage of Theresa May needing the DUP to prop up her government, so we think they should act'.[63]

The Northern Irish people have not had a forum through which the issue of abortion and the implications of the severe restrictions on it in the state can be aired. Many joined the debate in the Republic via social media, asking not to be forgotten and bemoaning that they did not have a similar democratic opportunity to decide the issue. There have been calls for a referendum on the issue in Northern Ireland and this has been taken up by, among others, Breedagh Hughes, NI Regional Director of the Royal College of Midwives.[64] The response from the main DUP politicians does not indicate any change of heart or mind, with key members declaring their determination 'not to be bullied' and promising to 'redouble their efforts' to prevent any change to the law.[65] The Alliance for Choice in Northern Ireland insists that this position is 'out-of-step' with public sentiment on the issue[66]; on 31 May 2018, women

[62]'Cross-Party Letter Calls for Change in NI Abortion Laws', *RTÉ News*, 22 July 2018, https://www.rte.ie/news/ulster/2018/0722/980290-abortion/, accessed 30 August 2018.

[63]Ibid.

[64]M. Berer of International Campaign for Women's Right to Safe Abortion, 'Northern Ireland—"The North Is Next"—Proposals Put Forward to Try and Make This Happen', http://www.safeabortionwomensright.org/northern-ireland-the-north-is-next-proposals-put-forward-to-try-and-make-this-happen/, accessed 5 September 2018.

[65]These were comments made by DUP members Ian Paisley Jnr and Jim Wells. Cited in K. Cooper, 'After Ireland Said Yes to Abortion, What Next for Northern Ireland?', *BBC News*, https://www.bbc.com/news/uk-northern-ireland-44271876, accessed 5 September 2018.

[66]Ibid.

protesting outside the High Court in Belfast held banners which read: 'We won't be left behind!'[67]

For now, in Northern Ireland abortion continues to be exported despite international condemnation. In November 2015 the High Court in Belfast ruled that Northern Ireland's abortion law violated the European Convention on Human Rights as it denied abortion for FFA and for cases of rape and incest; in the following month the court made a 'formal declaration of incompatibility'.[68] As noted, in 2016 the inter-departmental working group on abortion was established in Northern Ireland. Headed by the Chief Medical Officer for Northern Ireland, Michael McBride, this highlighted a move towards the medicalisation of abortion reform in Northern Ireland. However, at the time of writing, its consideration is still delayed due to the continued suspension of Northern Ireland assembly. For those opposing abortion law reform that may be opportune: the inter-departmental working group recommended that terminations for FFA be permitted in Northern Ireland. The report also engaged with Sarah Ewart's experience of having to travel from Northern Ireland to England after an FFA diagnosis in 2013 which emphasised: 'The trauma for [a] woman of travelling away from home and family at such a difficult time, the loss of her dedicated medical team and the associated financial cost'.[69] However, while Northern Ireland remains without a government, many of the women of Ireland are talking across borders and abortion is central to those conversations.[70]

[67] Berer, 'Northern Ireland—"The North Is Next"'.

[68] Dyer, 'Abortion Numbers Halve in Northern Ireland as Doctors Fear Prison', p. 135. A declaration of incompatibility rules that a statute is incompatible with the European Convention of Human Rights under the Human Rights Act 1998, section 4. See, Department of Justice and Department of Health, *Report of the Working Group on Fatal Fetal Abnormality: Healthcare and the Law on Termination of Pregnancy for Fatal Fetal Abnormality* (11 October 2016).

[69] 'Report Recommends Change to Strict Abortion Law in Northern Ireland', *RTÉ News*, 25 April 2018, https://www.rte.ie/news/ulster/2018/0425/957137-abortion-northern-ireland/, accessed 5 September 2018.

[70] There have been many imaginative methods used to cross these borders, including drones sent from the Netherlands with abortion pills to Northern Ireland. Berer of International Campaign for Women's Right to Safe Abortion, 'Northern Ireland—"The North Is Next"'; M. Davey, '"North Is Next": Fresh Fight for Grassroots Power That Beat Ireland Abortion Ban', *Guardian*, 1 June 2018, https://www.theguardian.com/world/2018/jun/02/north-is-next-fresh-fight-for-grassroots-power-that-beat-ireland-abortion-ban, accessed 30 August 2018; 'After Ireland's Abortion Vote the North Should

Conclusion

Media coverage of tragic cases such as Savita Halappanavar as well as legal challenges and prosecutions helped bring the 'woman's story to life', but as Sarah Ewart's case revealed, one of the most significant recent developments is women's willingness to speak of their abortion experiences and reject the culture of shame and silence.[71] This has been incredibly powerful and has resulted in the most sustained and open conversation on the island of Ireland regarding the meaning of abortion travel and women's reproductive health and rights. It also effectively allowed people to appreciate that there is no one type of woman that has an abortion; these were the 'real women' of Simon Harris's narrative.[72] We have now heard stories from or about teenagers, married couples, some with children, middle-aged women, rape survivors and refugees.[73] Engaging with this more nuanced view of the Irish abortion journey is a crucial step in creating an environment receptive to reform. It therefore took the words of women who had experienced abortions for a gamut of reasons to change the popular perception of them as incapable of making vital decisions about their own health and welfare.

Be Next', *Financial Times*, 27 May 2018, https://www.ft.com/content/331cc330-6009-11e8-ad91-e01af256df68, accessed 2 September 2018.

[71] Fox and Murphy, 'Irish Abortion: Seeking Refuge in a Jurisprudence of Doubt and Delegation', p. 455.

[72] Minister for Health, Simon Harris, 'Report of the Joint Committee on the Eighth Amendment of the Constitution: Statements', *Dáil Eireann Debate*, 17 January 2018, https://www.oireachtas.ie/en/debates/debate/dail/2018-01-17/25/, accessed 5 September 2018.

[73] Of Irish women having terminations in England in 2012: 124 were teenagers, 32 of whom were under the age of 16; 750 women had at least one abortion previously; 2700 were 3 to 9 weeks pregnant; 690 were 10 to 12 weeks; 12% were 13 to 19 weeks and (3%) were 20 weeks, *Belfast News-letter*, 12 July 2013.

CHAPTER 8

Conclusion

Abstract This book traces the histories of both of the states on the island of Ireland highlighting similarities, differences and the ways in which they have played off each other in relation to women's reproductive health and sexuality. The conclusion summarises the insights this all-island historical assessment of the Irish abortion journey has yielded. It argues that both states were conservative and shot through with fundamentalism across the religious spectrum until the 1960s. They were both only able to maintain their moral intransigence because Britain provided an abortion escape route. Ironically, both states held deep misconceptions about each other, but also used ideas of the other to play domestic politics often at the expense of women on the island. There are also significant differences in their responses to abortion, which lie in their differing relationship to Britain and their varying political structures, in particular the Republic's penchant for referendums, which created a vital civic space for transformative debate. In both states the role of women, both as abortion seekers and agents of social change, has been of central importance to the history of abortion and its reform.

Keywords Conservative states · Fundamentalism · Reform · Peace process · Mandate · Reform process

L. Earner-Byrne and D. Urquhart, *The Irish Abortion Journey, 1920–2018*, Genders and Sexualities in History,
https://doi.org/10.1007/978-3-030-03855-7_8

This book was prompted by the debates during the Republic's abortion referendum campaign and the reaction in Ireland to the overwhelming mandate delivered on 25 May 2018 to repeal the eighth amendment to the Irish constitution. Having worked on the history of sexuality and gender for much of our careers, we were keenly aware of the historical odds stacked against those campaigning for repeal, but we were also alert to the energy on the ground in Ireland in the weeks preceding the vote. However, nothing prepared us for the sight of women, young and old, in tears on the streets of Ireland on the days after the result or for the chanting of Savita's name outside Dublin Castle. The depth of the emotional response, its visceral nature, made us wonder if it was the weight of history shifting. We, therefore, began this book by asking ourselves two simple questions: first, what would historical context lend to our understanding of the Irish abortion journey? and secondly, how would our understanding of that history be enriched if we examined both jurisdictions on the island of Ireland?

We found, as expected, two conservative states shot through with fundamentalism across the religious spectrum. Both states were borne of violence and shaped by contested identities, but they shared not just the island but also its history. This meant in many ways that life on both parts of the island looked quite similar until the 1940s: poverty was rife, social inequality was entrenched, religion was central and authoritarianism was pervasive. For all these reasons women, welfare and rights were consciously and repeatedly subordinated to moral and religious concerns in both states for much of the twentieth century. Well-organised, well-connected and vocal, conservative groups yielded inordinate power, often brokering crucial issues relating to women's rights and autonomy behind closed doors. A common argument of these groups was that reproductive freedom, birth control and later abortion, harmed and demeaned women. This was an oft-recycled trope, even in Northern Ireland where birth control was never illegal, and it has been reiterated very recently in the Republic by Catholic Bishop Kevin Doran, who argued that contraception impinges on the 'dignity of women'.[1]

Both states held deep misconceptions about each other, but both also used ideas of the other to play domestic politics, often at the expense of women on the island. In the Republic, Northern Ireland was repeatedly

[1] C. Gleeson, 'Principles of Contraceptive Ban "Ignored for Too Long", Says Bishop', *Irish Times*, 4 August 2018.

portrayed as a haven of liberalism, while the North presented itself as morally superior to both the Republic and Britain. Peace politics and reproductive rights subsequently became entangled in complicated ways. On the one hand, southern politicians arguing in favour of legalising birth control in the 1970s suggested that this would appease unionist concerns regarding Irish reunification. On the other hand, those vehemently opposed to its legalisation were well aware that southern women were accessing birth control across the border. While all the main parties in the North shied away from confronting the issue of abortion, as the journalist Kenan Malik observed in 1994: 'Ironically, the current peace process may make it even harder to discuss the abortion issue. Both Catholics and Protestants cling to opposition to abortion as a piece of common ground between them. No politician on either side of the water wants to rock the boat'.[2] In consequence, those politicians chose to ignore the women leaving their shores to seek abortions elsewhere.

Both states therefore had much in common in their response to abortion: both exported it primarily to Great Britain and refused to provide clarity about when abortions could legally be performed within each state. This reluctance to provide guidance was likely bolstered by the suspicion that confusion favoured those who were opposed to abortion reform as doctors were more likely to err on the side of legal caution. Indeed, a recurring theme in this study is the way in which both states have used and/or attempted to use the courts, censorship and politics to deny women information and full autonomy in relation to their reproductive health. It is also clear that from the 1980s, both states were watching each other's abortion dramas unfold, keenly aware of their increasingly isolated positions internationally. Since the 1990s, in the courts on the island, the changing social mores and medical ethics played out often to the consternation of the public and women's groups. Yet, both states consistently ignored or refused to legislate based on the lessons of these cases.

There were also significant differences in the abortion histories of each state: since the 1980s the Republic has been constantly talking abortion with six referendums and several high-profile court cases. This penchant for referendums has provided a vital civic space for transformative debate about abortion. However, in Northern Ireland there has been no forum

[2] K. Malik, 'It's the One Thing That Unites Us'.

provided for public debate and, in fact, a concerted effort to keep the subject off the political radar with backroom deals and whispers of democratic crisis if the issue is forced from outside. On the ground, however, there is evidence that therapeutic abortions were, in practice, much more extensive than the letter of the law implied. Mark Benson, for example, has discovered research published in the *UMJ* in 1984, which indicates that during a rubella outbreak between 1978 and 1979, affected women were offered therapeutic abortions.[3] Furthermore, prior to the 2003 judicial review of Northern Irish abortion law in the High Court,[4] terminations for FFA were being performed in Northern Ireland.[5] Ironically, it was the agitation for clarification and guidelines that limited this option because, as a result of the judgment, the conditions for lawful abortion were defined much more narrowly.[6] Judge Sheil's ruling outlined: 'termination of a pregnancy based solely on the abnormality of the foetus is unlawful and cannot lawfully be carried out in this jurisdiction'.[7] This had an immediate chilling effect on the medical community in Northern Ireland. The sense of the net closing is clear in the consistently falling figures of therapeutic abortions in Northern Ireland and the prosecution of a young woman for procuring her own abortion in 2016. Hence, the repeal of the eighth amendment of the Irish constitution has inverted the narrative on conservatism on the island of Ireland. However, as this history underlines, these two states, often uncomfortable neighbours, do not exist in a vacuum and are constantly influencing and informing each other. The sight of Northern Irish women protesting

[3] Benson, 'The Provision of Abortion in Northern Ireland, 1900–1968', p. 245.

[4] In 2004, 'Family Planning Association of Northern Ireland v Minister for Health, Social Services and Public Safety', 8 October 2004.

[5] S. Ramshaw, 'Commentary on Family Planning Association of Northern Ireland v the Minister for Health, Social Services and Public safety', 1 August 2015; A. O'Donoghue, J. McCandless, and M. Enright (eds), *Northern/Irish/Feminist Judgments* (Oxford: Hart Publishing, 2016), Chapter 21. Available at SSRN https/ssrn.com/abstract=2847253.

[6] B. Hewson, 'The Law of Abortion in Northern Ireland', *Public Law* (Summer 2004), pp. 234–45, p. 235.

[7] Also see, Nicholson LJ paragraph 73 stated: 'it is unlawful to procure a miscarriage where the foetus is abnormal but viable, unless there is a risk that the mother may die or is likely to suffer long-term harm, which is serious, to her physical or mental health'. See, 'Family Planning Association of Northern Ireland v. The Minister for Health, Social Services and Public Safety Ref: 2004 NICA 39 Northern Ireland Court of Appeal (NICA)', 8 October 2004.

outside the high court in Belfast on 31 May 2018 carrying banners reading: 'We won't be left behind!' tells its own story.

Finally, throughout the history of this island the strength and endurance of women is a recurring truth. For much of the history of both states women operated underground in non-political ways: emigrating to secure adoption or abortion and as handywomen, helping other women 'in trouble'. The penalty for transgression was severe in both states; women were shunned, incarcerated and their children born outside of marriage sacrificed on the altar of morality. Until the 1970s women on this island had little control over their fertility: think of the women arriving at a Belfast hospital in the 1930s assuming they were entitled to have their 'periods brought on' and shocked to discover that continuing with a pregnancy was not a choice. Contemplate too, the women in Northern Ireland for whom internment offered a break in the cycle of relentless pregnancies. Or the mother of six in 1940s Dublin so desperate that she tried several times to secure a back street abortion only to eventually die of infection. Since the 1970s, women's groups have vocally championed reproductive freedom and sought to debunk a central myth that denying women control of their own bodies is not harmful to women. In both states the role of women, as abortion seekers and agents of social change, has been of central importance to the history of abortion and its reform. Ireland's abortion journey will diversify in 2019 as abortion law in the Republic is implemented, but this marks the start of a reform process rather than its end.[8]

[8] Singh, Remez, Sedgh, Kwok, and Onda, *Abortion Worldwide 2017 Uneven Progress and Unequal Access*, p. 19.

Selected Bibliography

Barry, Ursula, 'Abortion in Ireland', *Feminist Review*, 29 (1988), pp. 57–66.

Benson, M. T. S., 'The Provision of Abortion in Northern Ireland, 1900–1968'. Unpublished PhD thesis, Queen's University Belfast, 2017.

Bloomer, Fiona, and Kellie O'Dowd, 'Restricted Access to Abortion in the Republic of Ireland and Northern Ireland: Exploring Abortion Tourism and Barrier to Legal Reform', *Culture, Health and Sexuality*, 16: 4 (2014), pp. 366–80.

Compton, Peter, et al., 'Regional Differences in Attitudes to Abortion in Northern Ireland', *Irish Geography*, 19: 2 (July 1986), pp. 38–48.

Connolly, Linda, *The Irish Women's Movement: From Revolution to Devolution* (Basingstoke and New York: Palgrave, 2002).

Daly, Mary E., 'Marriage, Fertility and Women's Lives in Twentieth-Century Ireland (c.1900–c.1970)', *Women's History Review*, 15: 4 (September 2006), pp. 571–85.

———, *Sixties Ireland: Reshaping the Economy, State and Society, 1957–1973* (Cambridge: Cambridge University Press, 2016).

De Londras, Fiona, and Mairead Enright, *Repealing the 8th: Reforming Irish Abortion Law* (Bristol: Policy Press, 2018).

Delay, Cara, 'Pills, Potions, and Purgatives: Women and Abortion Methods in Ireland, 1900–1950', *Women's History Review* (2018), pp. 1–22. https://doi.org/1080/09612025.2018.1493138.

Farrell, Elaine (ed.), *'She Said She Was in the Family Way': Pregnancy and Infancy in Modern Ireland* (London: The Institute of Historical Research, 2012).

L. Earner-Byrne and D. Urquhart, *The Irish Abortion Journey, 1920–2018*, Genders and Sexualities in History, https://doi.org/10.1007/978-3-030-03855-7

Fletcher, Ruth, '"The Pro-Life" Absolutes, Feminist Challenges: The Fundamentalist Narrative of Irish Abortion Law 1986–1992', *Osgoode Hall Law Journal*, 36: 1 (1998), pp. 1–62.

———, 'Post-colonial Fragments: Representations of Abortion in Irish Law and Politics', *Journal of Law and Society*, 28: 4 (December 2001), pp. 568–89.

Fox, Marie, and Therese Murphy, 'Irish Abortion: Seeking Refuge in a Jurisprudence of Doubt and Delegation', *Journal of Law and Society*, 19: 4 (Winter 1992), pp. 454–66.

Francome, Colin, 'Irish Women Who Seek Abortions in England', *Family Planning Perspectives*, 24: 6 (1992), pp. 265–68.

Furedi, Ann (ed.), *The Abortion Law in Northern Ireland: Human Rights and Reproductive Choice* (Belfast: Family Planning Association Northern Ireland, 1995).

Girvin, Brian, 'An Irish Solution to an Irish Problem: Catholicism, Contraception and Change, 1922–1979', *Contemporary European History*, 27: 1 (2018), pp. 1–22.

Harding, Maebh, 'Irish Abortion Law—Legislating to Stand Still', *International Survey of Family Law*, 201 (2014), pp. 201–26.

Hesketh, Tom, *The Second Partitioning of Ireland?: The Abortion Referendum of 1983* (Dublin: Brandsma Books, 1990).

Hill, Myrtle, *Women in Ireland: A Century of Change* (Belfast: Blackstaff, 2003).

Holohan, Carole, *Reframing Irish Youth in the Sixties* (Liverpool: Liverpool University Press, 2018).

Hug, Crystal, *The Politics of Sexual Morality in Ireland* (Basingstoke and New York: Macmillan Press, 1999).

Jackson, Pauline, 'Outside the Jurisdiction: Irishwomen Seeking Abortion', in C. Curtin, P. Jackson, and B. Connor (eds), *Gender in Irish Society* (Galway: Galway University Press, 1987), pp. 203–23.

Maguire, Moira J., 'The Changing Face of Catholic Ireland: Conservatism and Liberalism in the Anne Lovett and Kerry Babies Scandals', *Feminist Studies*, 27: 2 (Summer 2001), pp. 335–58.

McAvoy, Sandra, 'The Regulation of Sexuality in the Irish Free State', in E. Malcom and G. Jones (eds), *Medicine, Disease and the State in Ireland, 1650–1940* (Cork: Cork University Press, 1999), pp. 253–66.

———, 'Before Cadden: Abortion in Mid-Twentieth-Century Ireland', in D. Keogh, F. O'Shea, and C. Quinlan (eds), *The Lost Decade: Ireland in the 1950s* (Cork: Cork University Press, 2004), pp. 147–63.

———, '"A Perpetual Nightmare": Women, Fertility Control, the Irish State, and the 1935 Ban on Contraceptives', in M. H. Preston and M. Ó hÓgartaigh (eds), *Gender and Medicine in Ireland, 1700–1950* (New York: Syracuse University Press, 2012), pp. 189–202.

McCormick, Leanne, '"The Scarlet Woman in Person": The Establishment of a Family Planning Service in Northern Ireland, 1950–1974', *Social History of Medicine*, 21: 2 (2008), pp. 345–60.

———, *Regulating Sexuality: Women in Twentieth-Century Northern Ireland* (Manchester: Manchester University Press, 2009).

———, '"No Sense of Wrongdoing": Abortion in Belfast 1917–67', *Journal of Social History*, 49: 1 (2015), pp. 124–48.

McGleenan, Tony, 'Bourne Again? Abortion Law in Northern Ireland After Re. K and Re. A', *Northern Ireland Legal Quarterly*, 45: 4 (Winter 1994), pp. 389–94.

Muldowney, Mary, 'Woman in Wartime: The Mass-Observation Diary of Moya Woodside', *The Irish Review*, 42 (Summer 2010), pp. 58–71.

Mullally, Una (ed.), *Repeal the 8th* (London: Unbound, 2018).

Oaks, Laury, '"Abortion Is Part of the Irish Experience, It Is Part of What We Are": The Transformation of Public Discourse on Irish Abortion Policy', *Women's Studies International Forum*, 25: 3 (2002), pp. 315–33.

Porter, Elizabeth, 'Culture, Community and Responsibilities: Abortion in Ireland', *Sociology*, 30: 2 (1996), pp. 279–98.

Qulity, Aideen, Sinead Kennedy, and Catherine Conlon (eds), *The Abortion Papers Ireland: Volume II* (Cork: Cork University Press, 2015).

Randall, Vicky, 'Irish Abortion Politics: A Comparative Perspective', *The Canadian Journal of Irish Studies*, 18: 2 (1992), pp. 107–16.

Rattigan, Clíona, 'Crimes of Passion of the Worst Character': Abortion Cases and Gender in Ireland, 1925–1950', in M. Gialanella Valiulis (ed.), *Gender and Power in Ireland* (Dublin: Irish Academic Press, 2008), pp. 115–40.

———, *What Else Could I Do?: Single Mothers and Infanticide, Ireland 1900–1950* (Dublin: Irish Academic Press, 2012).

Redmond, Jennifer, Sonja Tiernan, Sandra McAvoy, and Mary McAuliffe (eds), *Sexual Politics in Modern Ireland* (Dublin: Irish Academic Press, 2015).

Rose, R. S., 'Induced Abortion in the Republic of Ireland', *British Journal of Criminology*, 18: 3 (July 1978), pp. 253–54.

Rossiter, Ann, *Ireland's Hidden Diaspora: The Abortion Trail and the Making of a London-Irish Underground, 1980–2000* (London: Iasc, 2009).

Ruane, Medb, *The Irish Journey: Women's Stories of Abortion* (Dublin: Irish Family Planning Association, 2000).

Ryan, Louise, '"A Decent Girl Well Worth Helping": Women, Migration and Unwanted Pregnancy', in L. Harte and Y. Whelan (eds), *Ireland Beyond Boundaries: Mapping Irish Studies in the Twenty-First Century* (Dublin: Pluto Press, 2007), pp. 135–53.

Schweppe, Jennifer (ed.), *The Unborn Child, Article 40.3.3 and Abortion in Ireland: Twenty-Five Years of Protection?* (Dublin: Liffey Press, 2008).

Smith, Lisa, *Abortion and Nation: The Politics of Reproduction in Contemporary Ireland* (London: Ashgate, 2005).

Smyth, Ailbhe (ed.), *The Abortion Papers Ireland: Volume I* (Dublin: Attic Press, 1992).

Solomons, Michael, *Pro Life?: The Irish Question* (Dublin: Lilliput Press, 1992).

Stopper, Anne, *Mondays at Gaj's: The Story of the Irish Women's Liberation Movement* (Dublin: Liffey Press, 2006).

Index

L. Earner-Byrne and D. Urquhart, *The Irish Abortion Journey, 1920–2018*, Genders and Sexualities in History, https://doi.org/10.1007/978-3-030-03855-7

The manufacturer's authorised representative in the EU is Springer Nature Customer Service Centre GmbH, Europaplatz 3, 69115 Heidelberg, Germany. If you have any concerns regarding our products, please contact ProductSafety@springernature.com

Printed and bound by CPI Group (UK) Ltd, Croydon, CR0 4YY
11/10/2026
02231449-0001